# ——THE——
# RAW
# DEAL

## Also by Joe Conason

*The Hunting of the President: The Ten-Year Campaign
to Destroy Bill and Hillary Clinton*
(with Gene Lyons)

*Big Lies: The Right-Wing Propaganda Machine
and How It Distorts the Truth*

JOE CONASON

# THE

# RAW

# DEAL

## How the Bush Republicans Plan to Destroy Social Security and the Legacy of the New Deal

*Preface by James Roosevelt Jr.*
*Foreword by Al Franken*

PoliPointPress

The Raw Deal: How the Bush Republicans Plan to Destroy Social
Security and the Legacy of the New Deal
by Joe Conason

This edition published in 2005 in the United States of America
by PoliPointPress, P.O. Box 3008, Sausalito, CA 94966.
www.polipointpress.org

Production management: Michael Bass Associates
Copy editing: Laura Larson
Text design: Linda M. Robertson
Cover design: Wayne Kroenfeld

Library of Congress Cataloging-in-Publication Data

Conason, Joe
The Raw Deal/Joe Conason; preface by James Roosevelt Jr.,
foreword by Al Franken.
ISBN: 0-9760621-2-7

Printed in the United States of America
October 2005


Published by:
PoliPointPress, LLC
P.O. Box 3008
Sausalito, CA 94966-3008
(415) 339-4100
www.polipointpress.org

Distributed by Publishers Group West

*For my father—*
*who taught me the value of work*
*(and took me to get my Social Security card)*

# Contents

# THE RAW DEAL

# Preface

*by James Roosevelt Jr.*

**W**hen it comes to discussing America's most successful social program, mystification has become the order of the day. With pitiless repetition, we are told that Social Security is in crisis, that the program is unsustainable, and that it depends on meaningless IOUs for its funding. Earlier this year, we also heard that my grandfather, Franklin Delano Roosevelt, would have supported privatizing Social Security.

Taken together, these statements suggest that those who wish to privatize Social Security are the program's most loyal defenders. But even a brief review of the facts proves otherwise. Social Security is perhaps the most responsibly run part of the federal budget today. As the annual federal deficit balloons under President Bush's stewardship, the Social Security trust fund continues to rack up surpluses, as it will for years to come. The program is backed by its own revenue source as well as the full faith and credit of the United States government—the same full faith and credit that supports our currency, which Americans regard as very meaningful indeed. And most Americans recognize, even if the current administration does not, that a reliable form of social insurance is as important today as it was seven decades ago.

My grandfather didn't support privatizing Social Security, but at least three commentators—Brit Hume of Fox News, former Reagan official William J. Bennett, and *Wall Street Journal* columnist John Fund—claimed that he did. To support their arguments for privatization, all three misinterpreted a statement my grandfather made seven decades ago about a long-obsolete aspect of the program. When it became clear that they were torturing history, they stopped making that claim; but many who continue to call for privatization, from President Bush on down, have invoked the name of FDR. It's a compliment to him and the program's success, but it usually precedes an outrageous distortion.

Such distortions have become routine, but in this case, something very important is at stake. The New Deal, of which Social Security was an important part, helped set the stage for a long period of broad prosperity. It also helped "promote the general Welfare," a goal enshrined in the first sentence of the Constitution. Creating a system of social insurance was a difficult political achievement, but it has served this country well for seven decades. For all these reasons, most Americans take a dim view of attempts to dismantle it.

As *The Raw Deal* makes clear, our skepticism is justified. This book describes the most serious, well-financed, and determined effort to undo the

## Preface

Social Security Act since its inception in 1935. It also makes sense of the conflicting messages that bombard us daily. Above all, it shows who is behind the campaign to "reform" Social Security, what they hope to achieve, and how they are misrepresenting their goals. With devastating clarity, *The Raw Deal* exposes the faulty claims, deceptive methods, and ideological zeal of those who would "strengthen and protect" Social Security by weakening or abolishing it.

In this sense, *The Raw Deal* is a valuable contribution, but it's also a call to action. President Bush and his supporters have gone to great lengths to tout a costly and risky privatization plan, the details of which remain vague. But in the end, it will always fall to us, the American people, to protect our best social programs and promote the general welfare.

*James Roosevelt Jr. is an attorney, a former associate commissioner for retirement policy of the Social Security Administration, and a widely recognized expert on health care and insurance issues. He is currently president and chief executive officer of Tufts Health Plan, the pioneering New England health maintenance organization. A grandson of the late president Franklin Delano Roosevelt, he lives with his family in Cambridge, Massachusetts.*

# Foreword

*by Al Franken*

No one's a bigger fan of Social Security than I am. Unless you count my wife, Franni, whose father died when she was very little, and whose family never would have made it if it hadn't been for Social Security survivor benefits. So you can imagine the delight at the Franken household when we first learned that President Bush intended not only to "save" Social Security from an impending "crisis" but to "strengthen" it "for future generations."

Unfortunately, I wasn't able to pay any attention to the Social Security debate as it unfolded over the spring of 2005, because I was too busy hosting my three-hour daily radio show about politics and current events. I didn't have time to read the papers or watch any news on television. See, I used to operate under the theory that I'd be more effective on radio if I was fresh and unfettered by a whole bunch of useless information. If you don't like information, don't read this book. Because Joe Conason is the kind of guy who not only talks a lot, like me, but who also knows things.

Joe Conason is also the kind of guy who you'd want to invite on your show every Friday from 2 P.M. to 3 P.M. Eastern. But please don't. He's busy doing *my* show. And that's how I learned that Bush wasn't really trying to "strengthen" Social Security at all. He was trying to phase it out.

I know. It's hard to believe that President Bush would inaccurately characterize one of his own major policy initiatives. Even when Joe started explaining this, it took me several weeks to catch on. Not because Joe doesn't have a remarkable ability to distill complex political topics down to their fundamental core, and then explain that core with mordant wit and pitch-perfect moral opprobrium. No, the reason I didn't catch on was that I wasn't paying attention.

You see, by Friday afternoon, I'm exhausted, and when Joe arrives, I go on autopilot and just tune out. Usually, I'm thinking about what I'll do for the weekend. What celebrities I'm going to hang out with. What fancy restaurants I'll be seen at, dining with those celebrities. It's a lot to think about. And Joe is more than capable of carrying the ball.

But one day, Joe said something that caught my ear. As I was weighing the relative merits of Le Cirque with Sam Waterston or Nobu with the owner of Nobu, Joe said that the pro-privatization Alliance for Worker Retirement Security—which sounded to me like a group founded by labor unions—was actually a front group for a bunch of government-hating plutocrats. I'd always loved Disney cartoons, especially Mickey Mouse's wacky dog Pluto. (Many people think Goofy is Mickey's dog. They're full of it.) So when I heard "Pluto"-crats, I snapped to attention. That's when things started coming into focus. Bush's privatization plan, I learned, was an assault on the very foundation of America's social contract. For patriots, there could be no more urgent calling than its swift and total defeat.

I became insatiably interested in the subject, even to the point of starting to read again. It reminded me of the importance of staying informed. Not just as a citizen, but as a radio host. My show got much better. Also, I was able to understand everything Joe said, including previously confusing words like *benefits* and *risk*.

I learned how Social Security, unlike the country as a whole, wasn't really in crisis. At most, it had a very manageable solvency issue, one that could be solved in any number of ways. None of those ways, however, involved the creation of private accounts, or, as Bush would call them, "very personal accounts." Private accounts, it turned out, would involve "risk," which would undermine the "Security" part of Social Security. For a lot of people, that's their favorite part. Myself, I liked the "Social" part, because I'm a people person. But that's neither here nor there.

Joe told me that one way to solve the solvency issue would be to raise the cap on income that's subject to payroll taxes. I'm sure you'll find out more about that in this book. And probably Joe writes extensively about my own proposal: the "Al Franken Donut Hole." I don't want to bore you with a lot of numbers, but here's how it goes: We raise the cap to

$123,708. Why $123,708? Don't worry about that for now. OK. On income from $123,708.01 to $503,612, you don't pay any Social Security taxes at all. That's the Donut Hole. After $503,612, payroll taxes kick in again, but instead of 12.4 percent, you'll only pay 3.236068 percent, which math nerds out there will recognize as two times the Golden Mean. In this fashion, according to my back-of-the-envelope calculations, we can make up 81.91919191919 (repeating) percent of the projected shortfall. Anyway, that's the brief sketch. I'm sure Joe will flesh it out. If my plan is adopted, your grandchildren and their grandchildren's grandchildren will thank me and my Donut Hole.

In the part of the book not dedicated to explaining the Al Franken Donut Hole (which really does become more complex when you factor in dynamic scoring), you'll find a searing indictment of what is essentially a secret plot against the New Deal's greatest accomplishment. And it's also an exposé. What's the difference between an exposé and an indictment of a secret plot? You'll find that out, too, in my afterword. So enjoy the book. You'll be able to use what you learn here in debates, whether those debates occur at your high school cafeteria, at your nursing home cafeteria, or at Cafeteria, the fancy new restaurant recently opened by the owner of Nobu. I eat there all the time with Sam Waterston.

OK. I'll admit it. Sam's my only celebrity friend.

I know what you're thinking. "Joe Conason's a celebrity! A celebrity of the mind. Author of best-

# Foreword

sellers. Friday regular guest on America's best radio show." Thanks for the compliment! All that's true. So I guess you could say I have *two* celebrity friends. Or three, if you count Bob Balaban.

But even if Joe weren't my friend, I would recommend this book without having read it. Because I've read his other books. I trust this man. And because I think this is an important topic, even—no, especially—for people who won't need Social Security because they're incredibly rich. They'll be in positions of power, and they can make sure that Bush's plan doesn't come to fruition. I'm sorry, but that's the way it works in this country. Except for MoveOn.org. Hopefully, they'll change all that. But until then, money talks.

*Al Franken is a comedian, author, and host of* The Al Franken Show, *his daily three-hour radio broadcast (with Katherine Lanpher) on the Air America network. His bestselling books include* Lies and the Lying Liars Who Tell Them: A Fair and Balanced Look at the Right *and* Rush Limbaugh Is a Big Fat Idiot, *as well as the forthcoming* The Truth (with Jokes). *In 2003 he was a Fellow with Harvard University's John F. Kennedy School of Government at the Shorenstein Center on the Press, Politics, and Public Policy. He lives with his wife in New York City and Minnesota.*

# Introduction

In American salesmanship, the classic high-pressure strategy boils down to a pair of basic ploys. One seeks to create an intense feeling of urgency by warning us to "buy now, before it's too late!" The other tries to conjure a keen sense of opportunity by declaring whatever is on sale to be "new and improved!" Those old-fashioned slogans may sound corny, but the underlying techniques are still employed at all levels of marketing, even in the promotion of politicians and programs that the public would otherwise reject.

The aggressive sales force in the Bush White House has long since mastered modern marketing methods, using them to win elections and drive policy. They brought George W. Bush to power in 2000 by selling him as a new and improved "compassionate conservative."

Two years later, Bush's chief of staff candidly explained that war could be "rolled out"[1] on a publicity schedule, like any other product, to convince voters that action against Saddam Hussein's weapons of mass destruction was urgent. We had to invade—before it was "too late" to prevent catastrophe.

Everyone who paid attention has since learned that compassionate conservatism was nothing more than a happy-sounding phrase, and that those fearsome weapons of mass destruction were at best an exaggerated folly and at worst a total fraud. Yet the eventual emergence of the truth mattered little to the Republican pitchmen. In the absence of a vigilant, independent, and critical press, they were confident that their propaganda would always prevail.

Now they are applying the same methods of deception to their drive to destroy Social Security.

The president and his conservative allies tell us that they are offering a "new and improved"[2] version of America's most successful and efficient government program—and warning that we must buy their plan "before it's too late." They have spent many millions of dollars and invoked the prestige of the presidency, the Treasury Department, and the Social Security Administration to bulldoze Americans into buying their extraordinarily costly and risky privatization scheme. Social Security Administration officials have radically changed the agency's "communications strategy," from assuring workers that the program will be there when they retire to warning repeatedly that it is "unsustainable" and "underfinanced" and "must change." Their objective, financed by Social Security revenues, is to frighten the public into accepting Bush's "reforms."

# Introduction

Even the Social Security Administration's telephone hold message that greets citizens now includes propaganda messages along with the Muzak:

> Did you know that the seventy-six-million-strong baby boom generation will begin to retire in about ten years? When that happens, changes will need to be made to Social Security—changes to make sure there's enough money to continue paying full benefits. And most experts agree, the sooner those changes are made, the less they are going to cost.

In spring 2005, as voters learned about the trillion-dollar borrowing and enormous benefit cuts embedded in the president's proposal, the Bush administration's assault on Social Security stalled. Since then, many Republicans in the Senate and House have expressed open skepticism about passing any legislation that resembles the radical White House scheme, while the Democrats have remained unusually united in opposition. Congressional conservatives plan to revive privatization in the House of Representatives during the fall 2005 session and may pass private accounts in some form, but the Senate is unlikely to approve any such bill.

As the Bush initiative has foundered, right-wing publicists were forced to change the "branding" of his proposal yet again, having switched already from privatization to "partial privatization" to "personal accounts." The next buzz phrase was "progressive indexing."

So far none of the marketing and rebranding schemes has succeeded in moving the unfavorable poll numbers, which show about two-thirds of the American public opposed to any significant changes in Social Security.[3] If Bush's campaign has had any effect, in fact, it appears to have convinced more people to oppose privatization and to have inflicted damage on the president's own standing with the public. While most Americans realize that Social Security will someday require changes, their preferred solutions differ sharply from those offered by the president and his party. Not only do voters reject privatization, but they also want no part of benefit cutbacks, revised wage and price indexes, or delayed retirement. Instead, they strongly favor what the president dislikes most: increasing the cap on Social Security taxes above the current $90,000 level.[4]

Yet public resistance is unlikely to derail the privatization campaign, which traces back to the Reagan era as a quixotic crusade on the fringe of national politics. Having achieved so little for so long, the would-be privatizers now believe they have convinced the public that the program faces eventual ruin. With the president's determined support, they are spending tens of millions of dollars on propaganda—an effort that reflects a decade of preparation. If their campaign can persuade people that the system must be changed, a version of their destructive "reform" could eventually prevail.

Whether in government or out, the privatizers have sought to fabricate a "crisis" atmosphere and stoke irrational fears of "bankruptcy," amplifying the same themes that have been emphasized by right-wing groups and politicians for many years now. Thanks to generous corporate backing, they have established "Astroturf," or phony grassroots groups, to address senior citizens, African Americans, women, and young people. They have enlisted Republican consultants and donors to mount waves of television advertising.

The privatizers have mounted a nasty offensive against the American Association of Retired Persons (AARP), whose leaders dare to defend the interests of its thirty-three million members by opposing privatization. The spearhead of this attack is something called United Seniors Association, also known as USA Next, a creation of ultraright direct-mail impresario Richard Viguerie.

Viguerie has yearned to abolish Social Security ever since he joined the Goldwater presidential campaign in 1964. Under the United Seniors letterhead, he mailed out ominous, official-looking letters to the elderly, telling them that politicians have "spent all the money" in the Social Security trust fund. If they didn't contribute to United Seniors, their checks might be endangered.[5]

The current director of USA Next is a religious right activist and former Reagan administration official named Charlie Jarvis. He has vowed to expose the "liberalism" of AARP and "peel off" millions of its members to support the president's plan.[6] These days, Jarvis relies less on small contributions from elderly suckers and more on funding from major corporate interests such as drug and oil companies.

Indeed, the financial and political dimensions of the conservative effort to destroy Social Security—and dismantle the New Deal—are formidable. Arrayed behind privatization are the nation's largest and oldest corporate lobbying organizations; major Wall Street investment banks, oil companies, and pharmaceutical firms; top conservative foundations, renowned think tanks, skilled direct-mail organizations, and right-wing media outlets; and, of course, the Republican National Committee.

To some of these interests, a privatized social insurance and pension system represents a potential multibillion-dollar bonanza in contracts and fees. To others, it means an epoch-making ideological triumph over progressive values. Together, they are determined to achieve the victory that has eluded them for the past seventy years.

Much has changed in politics since Franklin Delano Roosevelt signed the Social Security Act on August 14, 1935, yet much remains surprisingly similar. FDR faced the unwavering hostility of the National Association of Manufacturers (NAM) and the United States Chamber of Commerce, which

President Franklin Roosevelt signs the Social Security Act in Washington on August 14, 1935. The bill provided old age pensions and unemployment insurance. From left are Chairman Robert Doughton (D-NC) of the House Ways and Means Committee; Senator Robert Wagner (D-NY), coauthor of the bill; Secretary of Labor Frances Perkins; Chairman Byron P. Harrison (D-MS) of the Senate Finance Committee; and Representative David L. Lewis (D-MD), coauthor of the measure. (© AP Photo)

now have renewed their determination to undo his domestic legacy.

Those powerful organizations have since come to understand that voters don't necessarily trust big business, so they hide their identity behind other names. Along with the Business Roundtable, a group of Fortune 500 companies, the U.S. Chamber and

NAM are promoting privatization behind two in-
nocuous-sounding fronts: the Coalition for the
Modernization and Protection of America's Social
Security (COMPASS) and the Alliance for Worker
Retirement Security (which sounds like it might
have been founded by the labor movement).

In Roosevelt's day, the Republican right lacked the
sophisticated "noise machine" that now dominates
American political discourse through talk radio and
cable television. The Heritage Foundation, the Cato
Institute, the Club for Growth, the American Enterprise Institute, the National Center for Policy Analysis,
and the Scaife, Olin, and Smith Richardson Foundations didn't exist back then. Despite all the changes
in technology and society that have occurred since
the Depression era, however, the fundamental interests and ideologies that were hostile to progressive change have scarcely changed since then.

In substance if not in form, the foundations and
organizations that have financed, conceived, and organized the campaign to phase out Social Security
bear a close resemblance to the old elites that bit-
terly opposed the New Deal.

As New Deal historian Kenneth Davis explains,
those titans of corporate power and wealth boasted
"a large control over mass communications . . . an
abundance of money with which to finance political
campaigns . . . and powerful legislative lobbies."[7] In
short, a situation not so very different from what we
now confront—except that the president and his

party have emphatically taken the side of the elites rather than the average citizen.

The top-hatted plutocrats who spat vitriol against Roosevelt—"that man" in the White House—suffered from an image problem that their ideological heirs have taken pains to repair. Today's privatizers represent the same interests as the program's old opponents—and a few, such as former Delaware governor Pete duPont and Richard Mellon Scaife, happen to be the direct descendants of FDR's ancient antagonists—but today they operate under friendlier-sounding names.

"Progress for America," for instance, is the well-heeled, White House–connected political committee that has sponsored some of the most frightening and misleading television commercials, which liken Social Security to the *Titanic* and predict that the program will "go bankrupt" if the president doesn't "rescue" it.[8] This outfit's financiers and masterminds are tied directly to Karl Rove—and include several of the Texas donors and Beltway consultants responsible for the scurrilous "Swift Boat" ads that targeted Democratic presidential nominee John Kerry in 2004.

Regardless of all the new labels and shifting slogans, however, the fundamental message of the Republican right has likewise remained essentially the same. From the beginning, conservatives combined cries of "crisis" with promises of "reform." They are constantly vowing to "save" the program they have always wanted to abolish.

Indeed, the notion that conservatives will save Social Security dates back to 1936, when Kansas Republican Alf Landon ran against FDR pledging to reform Social Security, which Landon denounced as a "hoax." The 1936 Republican Party platform flatly predicted that the federal government would be unable to pay retirement benefits to two-thirds of the elderly recipients, dismissed the Social Security program as "unworkable," and warned that "the fund will contain nothing but the government's promise to pay."[9]

That moldy old document sounds unmistakably like the current conservative line about the Social Security Trust Fund, which is said to contain "nothing but worthless IOUs."[10]

For more than two decades after Roosevelt's resounding victory over Landon, the opponents of Social Security were dismissed even within their own party. Among "modern Republicans" such as Senator Prescott Bush, the grandfather of George W. Bush, the prevailing viewpoint was that expressed by President Eisenhower in 1956. In a letter to his brother Edgar, Ike dismissed the ultraconservative opponents of the New Deal as "negligible" and "stupid."[11]

Eisenhower badly underestimated his adversaries on the right, as they proved eight years later when they returned from exile to seize control of the party behind Barry Goldwater. Among the extremist positions that excited the Arizona senator's followers was his plan to abolish Social Security by making participation "voluntary." He, too, believed that Social Security was foredoomed because "it promises more benefits to more people than the incomes collected will provide."[12]

The Goldwater campaign showcased a famous supporter who would go on to bigger things. On October 27, 1964, Ronald Reagan made his debut in national politics with a televised speech titled "A Time for Choosing," in which he devoted several minutes to an attack on Social Security. He warned of the program's "fiscal shortcomings" and denounced it as a "welfare program." He endorsed the Goldwater plan, which would have dismantled Social Security. (Reagan also tossed in a grim reference to France, which he said was about to be bankrupted by its commitment to national health insurance. "They've come to the end of the road," he intoned, in the voice that would later became so familiar.)[13]

Although voters repudiated Goldwaterism in a historic landslide, his movement laid the basis for the resurgence of the far right during the Reagan era and beyond. After Reagan entered the White House in 1980, he quickly abandoned his own prejudices about Social Security. Early on, ideologues in the Reagan White House floated a proposal to slash benefits, but congressional leaders of both parties instantly slapped down that idea. Several months later, Reagan appointed the bipartisan Greenspan Commission, named after its chairman Alan Greenspan, whose members urged increased payroll taxes, taxation of the benefits of upper-income retirees, expansion to cover millions of public employees, and increasing the assets of the Social Security Trust Funds. Those recommendations, signed into law by Reagan in 1983, ensured that the system could meet its commitments for at least sixty years.

An avowed admirer of FDR despite his own Republican conversion, Reagan ultimately ignored his right-wing clique and acted to preserve the New Deal legacy. At the same time, however, his presidency encouraged the resurgence of the far right—and thereby laid the foundations for George W. Bush's privatization campaign.

As president, Bush tipped his hand early on. Among his first initiatives, in May 2001, was naming a "Commission to Strengthen Social Security," which he duly stacked with supporters of privatization. Staffed by veterans of the Cato Institute, the corporate-backed libertarian group that has sought to dismantle Social Security for decades, the commission predictably issued "option papers" that plumped for private accounts.

Everyone understood that Bush's commission was rigged. Its credibility was almost nil—and whatever little enthusiasm its members managed to generate for privatization vanished entirely with the post-9/11, post-Enron stock plunge. Suddenly, the notion of turning the financial security of the nation's elderly and disabled over to the markets didn't seem so smart. Nor did it seem wise to emphasize privatization to a wary electorate that from left to right had always cherished Social Security. Republican congressional leaders began to step back from the president's notion during the midterm election of 2002, emphatically denying that they or their members had ever favored privatization.

Not much was heard from the Republicans on this sensitive subject until after the 2004 election, when they consolidated their control of the White House and Congress. Although Bush had vaguely reiterated his endorsement of private accounts during the campaign, he resolutely refused to detail any plan or even to explain how he intended to replace the trillions of dollars that even partial privatization would drain from the Social Security Trust Fund. In theory, he had been contemplating this critical "reform" for at least four years, but he still had nothing specific to offer.

When Bush commenced his barnstorming campaign for privatization during the late winter of 2004, he continued to avoid details. Instead, like a con man conjuring visions of easy money, he spouted promises that evaporated as the outlines of his plan began to leak from the White House.

So when the president predicted that everyone would earn lucrative returns on their "personal" accounts, he never mentioned the substantial risks or the management fees that would drain away income. When he pledged that each earner would control every dollar diverted from Social Security, he never mentioned that the investment choices would be strictly limited. And when he boasted that everyone would be able to will their privatized earnings to their heirs, he forgot to say that they would actually be required to purchase annuity plans that in most cases would leave little to be inherited.

Meanwhile, he warned again and again that someday soon, all the taxes Americans have paid toward Social Security during our working lives will disappear when the system suddenly goes "bankrupt." (Such alarming assertions contradict his administration's confident prediction of burgeoning growth, not to mention his promise to cut the federal deficit in half—but he and his advisers don't think anyone will figure that out.)

In short, the president is selling a "new and improved" deal that nobody could afford to turn down, although he grins coyly when anybody asks to see the fine print. And we must buy now, before it's too late.

In both style and substance, the Bush plan resembles a massive consumer fraud. Should he and his fellow salesmen succeed, the most likely result is a national case of buyer's remorse that will last for decades. But if Americans understand the real origins and goals of these "reforms," they are unlikely to buy into the raw deal.

# 1

# What the Bush Republicans Really Want

Over the past four decades, the strategy and tactics of American conservatism have changed much more than conservative ideology. What the Republican right currently advertises as "new ideas" are scarcely different from ideas that were already stale in 1964, but the advertising and public relations techniques used to sell them are far more sophisticated, smooth, and modern than the primitive, confrontational style of the past.

Today's Republican strategists understand that selling their social and economic agenda requires optimistic promises and inclusive rhetoric—and as a result they have taught their publicists, politicians and pundits how to repeat those soothing phrases in perfect chorus. Conservatives still hate Social Security—as did their ideological ancestors—but now they swear that they only want to "save" the system, not dismantle it.

In his day, their prophet Barry Goldwater was considerably more candid. The late Arizona senator

Senator Barry Goldwater accepts the Republican presidential nomination in San Francisco on July 16, 1964. Goldwater, the outspoken conservative Republican who served thirty years in the Senate, lost the presidency in a landslide. (© AP Photo)

was an old-fashioned reactionary who forthrightly admitted that he wanted to abolish Social Security by making the system "voluntary." As a committed radical right-winger, he believed that government shouldn't be providing social insurance (or most other services), and he bluntly expressed those views when he ran for president. He would serve up no "compassionate conservative" mush.

"Extremism in the defense of liberty is no vice," he told the 1964 Republican convention, calling forth rapturous cheering and whistling.[1] It was Goldwater's forthrightness about his agenda that helped voters to decide swiftly and in overwhelming numbers that he shouldn't be president. He lost by the largest margin in American history, a record he held until 1972.

By the time Goldwater ran for president, no significant political figure had suggested abolishing Social Security for more than two decades. There had been fitful efforts to tamper with FDR's legacy in 1947, when the Republicans took back control of the House of Representatives. But President Truman had quashed that foray, which only helped him to win election the following year.

When Republicans returned to the White House in the fifties, after their long exile, it was under the leadership of former general Dwight D. Eisenhower. Sensible Ike was a World War II hero of distinctly moderate disposition, who felt little kinship with his party's right wing or its seething compulsion to undo the New Deal. In a 1954 letter to his brother Edgar Newton Eisenhower, the president wrote:

> Should any political party attempt to abolish Social Security, unemployment insurance, and eliminate labor laws and farm programs, you would not hear of that party again in our political history. There is a tiny splinter group, of course, that believes you can do these things. Among them are H. L. Hunt (you possibly know his background), a few other Texas oil

**17**

# THE RAW DEAL

Portrait of General Dwight D. Eisenhower, future president of the United States, in his office March 1, 1950, in New York City. (© Arnold Newman/Getty Images)

millionaires, and an occasional politician or businessman from other areas. Their number is negligible and they are stupid.[2]

Stupid or not, Dallas-based Haroldson Lafayette Hunt was then one of the wealthiest men in the world, and one of the most medieval in outlook. A Christian fundamentalist who financed the John Birch Society and other extremist groups, Hunt believed that in an ideal society, "the more taxes you pay, the more votes you get," and that any poor or sick person who received government assistance should be denied an old-age pension and prohibited from voting.[3] (His son Nelson Bunker Hunt has long been active and influential in funding both the Republican Party and the religious right.)

Eisenhower correctly understood the Hunt viewpoint and its influence among leading figures in Texas petroleum circles. He was wrong about their power, however, at least in the Republican Party, where they helped Goldwater to win the nomination.

Running for the U.S. Senate in Texas on the Republican ticket that year was George Herbert Walker Bush, who enthusiastically endorsed his party's presidential candidate and campaigned with him. Bush was an oilman himself. His Senate campaign was financed by a "handful of Texas oil millionaires,"[4] and his views were considerably to the right of his own father, Senator Prescott Bush of Connecticut, a moderately liberal Eisenhower man.

That November, along with Goldwater, George H. W. Bush went down to crushing defeat. It was a searing personal and political failure that reportedly brought tears to the eyes of his eldest son George W., who had been imbibing right-wing thought from Goldwater's *Conscience of a Conservative*—and who would someday drive the Republican Party further to the right than his father's generation ever imagined.

Many years would pass, however, before conservative Republicans again dared to articulate their hostility to Social Security with the candor of Goldwater and his then-spokesman, Ronald Reagan. So decisive was the 1964 rout that when the Republican right came to power under the banner of Reagan, they scarcely mentioned the sore subject of social insurance. In fact, Reagan felt obliged during his 1980 campaign to pledge that he would never curtail Social Security, a promise he honored as president.

Even when the Republicans regained control of Congress in 1994, led by Newt Gingrich, the question of Social Security remained moot. Gingrich certainly hoped to privatize the system someday, but he knew better than to say so publicly. Instead, the Georgian demagogue stuck to the usual opportunistic approach favored by congressional Republicans. He posed as a protector of retirement benefits, defending the elderly, widows, and orphans from spendthrift liberals and federal raids on the Social Security trust fund.

Only with a substantial majority in both the Senate and the House, and only with President Bush safely ensconced in the White House for a second term, have Republicans again become willing to mount a sustained assault on Social Security's foundations. Actually, many Republicans on Capitol

Hill remain quite reluctant to endorse the president's privatization scheme, no doubt worried that an outraged electorate would decide to throw them out in the midterm elections. They remember that two decades ago, the mere prospect of cutbacks in Social Security benefits cost the Republicans control of the Senate.

To calm those fears—and to help persuade voters that the Republican leadership means no harm to the system that has served the nation so well for so long—the renowned GOP pollster and consultant Frank Luntz stepped forward with detailed instructions.

In a lengthy memorandum prepared for congressional Republicans, Luntz painstakingly explains how to sell the president's plan to skeptical constituents. Just as he did when his advice helped Gingrich to attain power more than a decade ago—by urging Republican congressional candidates to stigmatize Democrats as "sick," "permissive" and "traitors"—Luntz now instructs Republicans on what to say about Social Security, word for word and sentence by sentence.

The basic lessons taught by Luntz are simple enough for any member of Congress to comprehend. He has found that certain words and phrases poll much less favorably than others. That is why Republicans—paying careful attention to Luntz—have abandoned the term *privatization* after decades of using that term to describe what they would do to Social Security. Relying on research that consistently shows majority opposition to private accounts, Luntz exhorts them never to use that word again.

"If necessary, do what I do and institute a strict policy among your staff that anytime someone uses either 'privatize' or 'individual' in the context of Social Security, they must pay you $50," he urges. "It works."[5]

Luntz instructs the congressional Republicans with sentences carefully designed to reassure their constituents. Sentences like "Americans have a right to a safe, secure retirement"; and "Current and near-retirees deserve peace of mind in knowing they will receive full benefits for their entire retirement"; and "We have a responsibility to save Social Security RIGHT NOW . . . so that our children and generations to come receive the same benefits we have enjoyed." According to Luntz, Republicans must always vow to "strengthen" and "protect" Social Security. Indeed, the list of "principles" he urges Republican politicians to articulate sound like lines lifted directly from old Democratic stump speeches.[6]

"Doctor Luntz," as he prefers to be known, is a living caricature of the morally hollow political consultant. He knows that the Bush plan for Social Security would not provide the "same benefits" that the system has delivered for the past seventy years. He also knows that the intense, ongoing effort by the Bush administration and its allies to create panic about the fiscal prospects of the Social Security system is not designed to foster anybody's "peace of mind."

Only the ultimate cynic could so breezily counsel incumbent Republicans to run against "Washington"—as Luntz does repeatedly in his memo—when their party controls the White House, the Senate, and the House of Representatives.

But Luntz is smart and his political instincts are sharp. Although much of what he tutors Republicans to say about Social Security is misleading, he certainly understands the implications of his polling.

And what he understands above all is that Republicans and conservatives have long suffered from their perceived hostility to Social Security. On that point he offers a clear warning: "If Americans think you want to protect and enhance their retirement security, they'll back you," he writes. "If they think you want to reduce their benefits—for *any* reason—they'll oppose you."[7]

So Luntz tells his GOP pupils that they must promise to "strengthen" Social Security. Those promises *sound* reassuring, and whatever sounds good is what matters to the Republican pollster. Plain truth is not his stock in trade. Among many other distinctions, after all, he is the linguistic manipulator who came up with a name for the Bush administration's plan to undermine air pollution regulations: it was called the "Clear Skies Initiative."

While most Republicans and conservatives have observed "strict message discipline" on Social Security, as Luntz observes with satisfaction, the old desire to abolish the program and every vestige of the New Deal still surfaces from time to time like a Freudian slip. For most of the individuals and organizations involved in the Bush drive for privatization, that desire remains the most important ideological motivation. They may force themselves to praise Social Security, but they have really come to bury it.

Despite the savvy advice of propagandists like Luntz, the deep hostility of the privatizers still emerges at the most inconvenient moments.

Consider what happened to Senator Rick Santorum, the Pennsylvania Republican who ranks third in the Senate majority leadership, when he held a series of "town hall meetings" on Social Security in late February 2005. An ardent privatizer and ultraconservative who is up for reelection in 2006, Santorum found himself confronted by hostile audiences all over the state who let him know they wanted no part of the Bush plan.

That was annoying, of course, but the worst publicity came from a group of College Republicans who showed up to rally for Santorum at Drexel University in Philadelphia.

As the senator entered the school's auditorium, with radio and television reporters recording the moment, the young conservatives could be heard chanting, "Hey hey! Ho ho! Social Security's got to go! Hey hey! Ho ho! Social Security's got to go!" The senator smiled wanly at this embarrassing display of youthful zeal.

Such sentiments aren't only to be found among the right-wing young. Last May, the same kind of indiscreet candor emerged during a conference hosted in New York by the Cato Institute. The Washington-based libertarian think tank—ideological spearhead of the drive to privatize Social Security for more than two decades—had invited hundreds of conservative activists and business leaders to hear speeches and panel discussions on the president's plan.

The speakers included Cato president Ed Crane, who published the first book promoting Social Security privatization in 1982, and Michael Tanner, who directs Cato's Project on Social Security Choice (once known, pre-Luntz, as the Project on Social Security Privatization). Among the distinguished guests were Jose Piñera, the former labor minister of Chile, who oversaw the privatization of that country's social insurance system during the Augusto Pinochet dictatorship, and Bush economic adviser Allan Hubbard, who concluded the conference with a luncheon address.

Hubbard opened his remarks by praising Cato as "important to our country and our world," and he went on to make the best case he could for the Bush administration's management of the economy.[8] The audience of investment bankers and conservative activists was not impressed with the bromides and statistics offered up by Hubbard, named by Bush to head the National Economic Council in January 2005.

A car wax magnate from Indianapolis who once served as deputy chief of staff to Vice President Dan Quayle—and, more important, an old pal of George W. Bush from Harvard Business School—Hubbard certainly shares the president's conservative ideology as well as his dim view of Social Security. Back in 1988, Hubbard managed the mercifully brief presidential campaign of former Delaware governor Pierre S. duPont IV, the Republican chemical and banking heir who was the first presidential candidate to propose replacing the program with private accounts.

At the Cato luncheon Hubbard gave a gushing tribute to Piñera, who has devoted his life to privatizing Social Security programs worldwide: "Jose has been my hero forever. . . . I admired what he did for Chile."

Yet although none of this ingratiating palaver won much approval from the tough Waldorf audience, they began to clap wildly as soon as they heard this question addressed to Hubbard: "The Social Security program is close to 25 percent of the federal budget. What better opportunity could there be for the government to phase out Social Security? Why can't we do that?" the questioner demanded, his voice rising. "The federal government has no business in retirement."

When the roar of applause subsided, Hubbard quickly reverted to the official White House line. "The President very much believes in Social Security," he insisted. "The President's goal is to preserve

Social Security. . . . He is opposed to privatizing Social Security. . . . He is totally committed to preserving the system. . . . Social Security needs to be fixed."

In that room, Hubbard was lucky not to be booed for such a mealy-mouthed answer. The men who run the Cato Institute emphatically *do not* believe in Social Security, which they have branded "a Ponzi scheme," "a pyramid scheme," "a bad deal," "an incredibly bad investment," and "a cancer."[9]

Under the tutelage of Frank Luntz, however, they try not to talk that way any more. They speak only of "choice" and personal accounts, and never of privatization.

Cato's insiders understand that while the president and his advisers cannot speak too frankly—and in fact must always blather on about saving and protecting and strengthening—they are equally eager to "phase out" Social Security. To understand what lies beneath the presidential rhetoric of "protecting" and "strengthening" Social Security, it is useful to inspect the determined ideologues surrounding the president and his top advisers. Their real purposes can be discerned from the political company they keep.

Setting the mood for the administration during its early months were Paul O'Neill, the new Treasury secretary, and Lawrence Lindsey, the Bush campaign economics tutor who was named as chairman of the White House's National Economic Council.

Lindsey was a protégé of Martin Feldstein, the conservative Harvard economist and Bush adviser who has devoted a significant part of his career to undermining Social Security and promoting privatization. True to his mentor, Lindsey soon devised a plan for private accounts "based on creative accounting principles," as journalist Ron Suskind explained.[10] He proposed that the government incur trillions in debt to pay Social Security benefits, so that revenues could be diverted into private accounts. The debt would be serviced by clawing back a substantial portion of the anticipated returns from the new "personal accounts." This mathematically unworkable idea became known among earthbound economists as the "free lunch" scheme.

As for O'Neill, the outspoken, extremely wealthy former chairman of Alcoa Corp. confided his true feelings about Social Security and other matters during an interview with *Financial Times* columnist Amity Shlaes in May 2001.

Explaining back then why he believes both Social Security and Medicare ought to be abolished, along with corporate taxes, O'Neill told Shlaes, "There's a concept that has a lot of appeal to me. Able-bodied adults should save enough on a regular basis so that they can provide for their own retirement and for that matter for their health and medical needs."[11]

When a columnist for a New York newspaper called the Treasury Department to check the secretary's quotes, a spokesman assured him that O'Neill had been quoted accurately. The White House didn't bother to issue a rebuke or disclaimer, although two years later O'Neill was booted out of his job for other offenses. He may be gone, but the strongly negative attitude he articulated toward social insurance still remains.

That attitude is what unites the Bush White House with the conservative experts and activists who have joined its campaign to "reform" Social Security. More than any professed concern about fiscal prudence or generational equity, the Bush Republicans are motivated by their profound ideological hostility to the progressive legacy of the New Deal.

Telltale clues to their true aims can be found in the "crisis" that these conservatives have chosen to address and the "solution" they are promoting. There is in fact no imminent crisis in Social Security financing, and if economic growth continues as it has in the past, there won't be. If growth slows slightly over the next few decades, then Social Security may require additional revenues or benefit adjustments, but the potential problems are comparatively small and easily fixed. If growth slows enough to endanger Social Security, then the equity returns projected under privatization schemes will be impossible.

As the economist Paul Krugman has explained, more difficult and immediate problems loom in the outsized deficits created by the Bush tax cuts, and in the rapid inflation of medical costs that threatens Medicare and Medicaid.[12]

If the Bush Republicans were honestly worried about the economic effects of deficits and debt, they would consider repealing or reforming Bush's lopsided tax cuts. If they were truly troubled by issues of generational equity, they would be dealing with the burgeoning costs of Medicare (which Bush's opportunistic "reforms"—including his impossibly complicated prescription drug benefit—have only made worse).

And if the Bush Republicans wanted to ensure Social Security's future solvency, they wouldn't insist on private accounts carved out of its revenue stream—which will only increase the program's eventual deficit. Their priorities show that the real goal of the Bush Republican "reform" campaign is to phase out Social Security altogether. But then these are radical right-wingers, whose feelings about government, the New Deal, and the legacy of FDR are far outside the American mainstream.

Their radicalism is exemplified by Grover Norquist, the most important political operative outside the White House, whose official title as president of an obscure "tax reform" group belies his central role in coordinating conservatives in the nation's capital. Norquist, who entered politics as part of a rightist cabal that seized control of the College Republicans, has long presided over a Wednesday morning meeting that attracts representatives from more than eighty conservative organizations, including right-wing media outlets, as well as staffers from the White House and Congress.[13]

As former conservative insider David Brock explains, the Wednesday morning group convenes "to set movement priorities, plan strategy, and adopt talking points." In that vein, Norquist works very closely with White House deputy chief of staff Karl Rove.[14]

According to Brock, the members of this motley coalition are brought together by their mutual desire to "roll back the economic and social gains made in the country since the New Deal."[15]

Or, as Norquist himself once quipped, "Our goal is to cut government in half as a percentage of the economy over twenty-five years, so that we can get it down to the size where we can drown it in the bathtub."[16]

That aspiration has never stopped Norquist from using his proximity to government to earn money for himself and his organization, both as a registered lobbyist and as a purveyor of "access" to the Bush White House. He arranged meetings with the president and Karl Rove for Indian tribal casino interests that had donated $1.5 million to Norquist's organization, Americans for Tax Reform.[17]

Norquist looks back fondly on the 1920s, when the federal government did almost nothing to help its citizens and therefore spent only 3 percent of the nation's gross domestic product. That's a prescription for the cyclical depressions and mass poverty suffered by past generations, a prospect that apparently doesn't trouble him.

With Social Security accounting for about one-fourth of annual government expenditures, Norquist would be unlikely to achieve his ambitious goal of cutting government "in half" if the program survives. (No doubt that is why Americans for Tax Reform hired Peter Ferrara, an attorney and author of the first Social Security privatization plan in 1980, as its "chief economist" several years ago.)

While Americans for Tax Reform faxes press releases touting its plan to "strengthen" Social Security with personal accounts, its president spoke more candidly at the January 2004 Conservative Political Action Conference in Washington. There he declared that his "leave us alone coalition"— Americans who own guns and who educate their children at home or in private schools—have rejected government and want to "eliminate" Social Security and other entitlement programs.

When George W. Bush spoke about Social Security as a presidential candidate in 2000, he called it "the single most successful government program in history." He promised to "lock away more than $2 trillion of the federal surplus" to finance the program's future benefits, and he swore to stop Washington politicians from dipping into the Social Security trust fund. He repeatedly said that he would seek a "bipartisan consensus" for any changes in the program. He said that he would "fix" Social

Security and ensure that the system remained "strong and financially secure for America's children and grandchildren."[18]

In hindsight, the sincerity of Bush's vows can be judged by how swiftly he has violated them. As president he proceeded to turn the federal surplus left by Bill Clinton into an endless series of deficits by doling out enormous tax cuts to the wealthiest 1 percent of American citizens, and he has since siphoned hundreds of billions of dollars from the trust fund every year to make those deficits look smaller.

Among Beltway conservatives, it is no secret that the president's reassuring rhetoric serves to camouflage goals he cannot proclaim openly. After Bush won the Republican nomination in 2000, the venerably conservative *National Review* published a candid assessment of what he really means when he talks about "strengthening" Social Security and what is at stake:

> What Bush is saying is that this relic is no longer sacrosanct. . . . Over time, public pressure to let workers invest 3 percent—then 4, then more—would be irresistible. Opponents of reform have darkly suggested that private accounts, if introduced on a small scale, will eventually completely replace Social Security. They are quite correct, though they are wrong to see this as a Wall Street plot. . . .

> If enacted, [privatization] would put within reach many conservative goals for America that can now scarcely be conceived of.[19]

After seventy years, phasing out Social Security still remains the most important domestic objective for Republicans and conservatives. For them it is a simple question of ideology and power—and they don't worry about the risks that their gamble would impose on the rest of us.

## 2

# The President's Commission to Privatize Social Security

**W**henever the president of the United States appoints a blue-ribbon commission, the stated purposes are to illuminate an important and complex national problem, evaluate proposed solutions, and present a program of government action that is likely to be both effective and broadly accepted. Almost always, however, the unstated purpose is to provide the impetus for fearful elected officials to do something, perhaps something potentially unpopular, and to do it together—which means reaching a consensus that is moderate, mainstream, and genuinely bipartisan.

To attain credibility and ultimate success, such commissions require diverse and widely respected appointees, professional nonpartisan staff, and a determination to find solutions that will, to paraphrase George W. Bush, unite rather than divide.

All those qualifications would appear to be particularly critical for a panel asked to address sensitive questions concerning the future of Social Security, a vast and vital program that affects every American family. The Greenspan commission appointed by Ronald Reagan in 1981 to ensure Social Security's solvency met all those criteria, in large part because the president consistently acted in cooperation with the Democratic congressional leadership when dealing with the panel and its recommendations.

Although he proclaims his admiration for the late Reagan, George W. Bush is different—in both his determination to impose radical right-wing ideology and his disdain for bipartisan cooperation. Bush departed from the traditional blueprint even before the White House officially announced the formation of the "President's Commission to Strengthen Social Security" on May 2, 2001.

His press secretary Ari Fleischer set the tone the day before the president appeared in the Rose Garden with the members of his new commission. Word about the panel had already leaked out, and the reaction wasn't favorable. Everyone knew that although the personalities named to the commission were selected to present a tableau of diversity—including blacks, Hispanics, women, and Democrats as well as the usual white male Republican suspects—all were proponents of privatization. Nobody in the White House had asked the Democratic congressional leaders for their opinion.

Ever in character, Fleischer spoke as if stacking the commission to reach predetermined conclusions were the only natural thing for the president to do.

"The commission that the president will announce will, of course"—of course!—"be comprised of people who share the president's view that personal retirement accounts are the way to save Social Security."[1] No skeptics needed apply.

Looking back, Bush's attitude toward Social Security can be traced to his first unsuccessful campaign for elected office. Running for Congress in his hometown of Midland, Texas—then and now one of the most right-wing districts in the Lone Star State—he stood up at the local country club and warned his audience of real estate agents that Social Security "will be bust in ten years unless there are some changes." According to a report in the local newspaper, he went on to suggest that the "ideal solution would be for Social Security to be made sound and people given the chance to invest the money the way they feel."[2]

As the *New York Times* observed, what Bush said in Midland a quarter-century ago differs little from what he said when traveling around the country in 2005 (and as the *Times* didn't observe, his remarks continue to lack both specifics and accuracy).

His first exposure to the privatization scheme may have come when, as a prep school student, he read Barry Goldwater's 1963 declaration of principles, *The Conscience of a Conservative*. Al Hubbard, who attended Harvard Business School with Bush and currently serves as a White House economic adviser, told the *New York Times* that privatizing

Social Security "was never a new idea. It was always there, like tax cuts."[3]

It was always there indeed—and long before Bush ever thought about the issue—at least in the fever wards of the far right. As a serious proposal, however, abolishing or privatizing Social Security had never much extended beyond that political quarantine.

The breakout began in the late 1970s and early 1980s with the rise of a new generation of well-financed, publicity-savvy policy entrepreneurs on the right. With millions in steady annual funding from several major conservative foundations—including those operated by the Coors, Scaife, Smith Richardson, and Olin families—those entrepreneurs created new institutions such as the Heritage Foundation and the Cato Institute to refurbish, remodel, and market their ideas.

The pedigree of these organizations varied, as did their ideology. Created largely with Coors money and tinged in its early years by unsavory connections with racist and fascist extremists, Heritage reflected the ideology of the hard-right Taft–Goldwater wing of the Republican Party—the crowd that had never accepted Eisenhower's "modern Republicanism." Paul Weyrich, the former Capitol Hill aide who first headed Heritage (and went on to become an eminent leader in conservative Washington), used to reminisce about his Wisconsin youth, when his parents would listen faithfully to the radio broadcasts of Father Charles Coughlin, the anti-Semitic demagogue and venomous enemy of the New Deal.[4]

The Cato Institute arose from similar although not identical ideological extremism. Its founding patrons were heirs of the Koch industrial clan of Kansas, whose patriarch Fred Koch had been a charter member and financial backer of the paranoid, ultraright John Birch Society (the society's founder Robert Welch once accused President Eisenhower of being a Communist agent).[5]

Fred's oldest son Charles was attracted in his youth to the fringe politics of the Libertarian Party, where he met Ed Crane, a party activist with a larger vision. Frustrated by ineffectual third-party antics, Crane was determined to establish a new think tank that could achieve respectability and influence for libertarian ideas. In 1976, Charles Koch gave Crane $500,000 in seed money to create Cato.

Both Heritage and Cato now operate out of their own imposing Washington buildings, with multimillion-dollar budgets and hundreds of employees sending out thousands of papers, publications, and press releases annually on foreign and domestic issues. Although Heritage advocates traditional religious morality while Cato favors sexual freedom—among other differences—their views usually converge on economic issues.

On matters of taxation, regulation, and social welfare, the core attitude of Heritage and Cato is that the state does almost nothing right and private industry rarely does anything wrong. Liberty will survive and prosperity flourish only under minimal government. Social insurance and consumer protection are not only inefficient but morally wrong. Armed with those certainties, the researchers and scholars hired by Heritage and Cato tend to be highly predictable. In nearly three decades of research on hundreds of topics, their "scholars" have rarely discovered any data that conflict with those prejudices.

Happily, if not coincidentally, those very same prejudices mesh quite neatly with those of the institutions' most generous patrons. Charles Koch and David Koch, for instance, have donated upward of $20 million to the Cato Institute over the past three decades through their three family foundations. Their family firm is the second-largest privately held company in America and the nation's largest privately held energy firm. Like most billionaires, the brothers dislike taxes, and they are also profoundly hostile to government regulation—no doubt because Koch Industries has so often run into costly trouble over pollution, taxes, and petroleum taken illegally from Indian lands.

The roster of Cato sugar daddies has expanded well beyond a few wealthy eccentrics to include many of the nation's largest corporations, again because those corporate entities have found a happy coincidence between Cato studies and their own perspectives. From the energy sector, Cato has enjoyed the generosity of Chevron, Exxon Mobil, Shell, and Tenneco, along with the Amoco and Atlantic Richfield Foundations and the American Petroleum Institute.

Their tax-deductible investment returns pure intellectual profit. Typical selections from Cato's scholarship on the subject of energy and the economy include "Climate of Fear: Why We Shouldn't Worry about Global Warming," a two-volume study of oil and gas regulation that purportedly proves "good intentions led always to economic waste with no offsetting social gain," and an essay by Cato chairman William Niskanen that urges the repeal of "all federal environmental legislation enacted since 1972."[6]

That kind of sweeping generalization isn't unusual at Cato, where rigorous enforcement of the party line ensures uniformity of opinion. Most government spending should be cut, most government agencies should be abolished, most regulations ought to be repealed, most taxation should be cut, and most federal activity should be pruned back—including the military. On certain issues, such as foreign intervention, homosexual rights, and drug policy, Cato might be considered radically left. It vehemently opposed the U.S. invasion of Iraq, and it has urged the legalization of narcotics, including cocaine and heroin. Cato vice president David Boaz is a veteran gay rights advocate who believes the government should play no part in sanctioning marriage, and the institute has spoken out strongly against the Federal Marriage Amendment that would ban gay marriage.

Advocacy of drug legalization and gay rights may be unorthodox on the right, but those aspects of libertarian philosophy don't seem to disturb the institute's corporate sponsors. Cato maintains mutually beneficial relationships with many of the nation's largest businesses, including the pharmaceutical industry, the financial industry, and even the tobacco industry, with big donations from Philip Morris and R. J. Reynolds that helped finance the institute's attacks on antismoking legislation. It is amusing to read an essay by a Cato flack worrying about increased cigarette taxes because they are "terribly regressive"—a problem that rarely troubles conservatives in analyzing tax policy.[7]

Predictably, Cato also opposes most government regulation of the financial industry, preferring to allow "the incentive forces of private property rights to create competitive markets and to provide consumer information and protection."[8] If that sounds suspiciously like permitting unchecked growth of enormous agglomerations of corporate financial power that can easily devour uninformed and unprotected consumers, it could explain why the institute is lavishly supported by American Express, J. P. Morgan Chase Bank, Citicorp, Prudential Securities, and Salomon SmithBarney.

## The President's Commission to Privatize Social Security

As for Cato's effort to privatize Social Security, the most generous donor to the institute's Project on Social Security Privatization—rechristened the Project on Social Security Choice a few years ago—is American International Group (AIG), which happens to be the world's largest insurance company. AIG also just happens to manage privatized retirement systems in other countries, and it might well find itself in a position to profit from the establishment of a similar system in the United States. (In the meantime, however, the company finds itself in the midst of a financial scandal that led to the undignified ouster of Maurice "Hank" Greenberg, a major Republican donor and Bush family friend who had run AIG for almost forty years.)

Long before the corporate money began to pour in, however, the Cato Institute and the Heritage Foundation determined that their shared agenda—which eventually extended to include the rest of the conservative movement and the Republican Party—must include as a top priority the destruction of Social Security, both as a symbol of the hated New Deal and as an enduring success for progressive government.

In 1980, Cato president Ed Crane read a six-hundred-page paper proposing the privatization of Social Security, written by a Harvard Law School student named Peter Ferrara. Eager to encourage the idea, Crane published Ferrara's treatise as *Social Security: The Inherent Contradiction*, which became the Cato Institute's first book.

"Under traditional principles of equity," Ferrara wrote, "the social security compact between the generations is unfair, immoral, fraudulent, and voidable." Two years later, the Heritage Foundation published a second book by Ferrara on the same themes and hosted a conference in Washington called "Rebuilding Social Security."

By the following autumn, the two think tanks set forth a joint strategy paper on getting rid of Social Security, authored by Stuart Butler, director of domestic studies at Heritage, and Peter Germanis, a Heritage Social Security analyst, and published in *Cato Journal*. The authors' excitable tenor is evident in their unlikely source of inspiration. "Lenin recognized that fundamental change is contingent upon . . . its success in isolating and weakening its opponents," they wrote. "We would do well to draw a few lessons from the Leninist strategy."[9]

Their essay suggested a strategy of "what one might crudely call guerrilla warfare against both the current Social Security system and the coalition that supports it." This campaign was to entail "educational" efforts by major corporations, through "advertising and public relations," as well as efforts to reach "key figures in the media" with the privatization message.[10]

Writing in 1983, Butler and Germanis were deeply disappointed that the Reagan administration and Congress, following the recommendations of the Greenspan commission, had bolstered the

# The President's Commission to Privatize Social Security

President Ronald Reagan signs the Social Security Act Amendment on April 20, 1983, with Vice President George Bush (far right), Senator Bob Dole (second from left), Congressmen Tip O'Neill (fourth from right), and Senator Daniel Moynihan (fifth from right) on hand as witnesses. (© *CORBIS*)

Social Security system by ensuring the solvency of the trust fund with new revenues and benefit changes. What they hoped was that a new conservative coalition would be in place when, sometime in the future, Social Security encountered a fiscal crisis. That might take a while, they acknowledged.

"Finally, we must be prepared for a long campaign. The next Social Security crisis may be further away than many people believe . . . [and] it could be many years before the conditions are such that a radical reform of Social Security is possible.

But then, as Lenin well knew, to be a successful revolutionary, one must also be patient and consistently plan for real reform."[11]

Meanwhile, however, the ideal conditions for "radical reform" akin to the model preferred by Heritage and Cato had already arisen in Chile—namely, the 1973 military coup that deposed the democratically elected socialist coalition government of Salvador Allende and replaced it with a dictatorship headed by General Augusto Pinochet. Eight years into the general's fifteen-year rule, his regime instituted a truly radical revamping of the Chilean social security system—the oldest in the Western Hemisphere—that encouraged workers to switch to private retirement savings plans. Overseeing the implementation of the Pinochet program was a young bureaucrat named Jose Piñera, who would eventually become the cochairman of Cato's Project on Social Security Privatization.

"They did have certain advantages in Chile," remarked Sylvester Schieber, an American pension consultant. "They did have a dictatorship and they did have control over the public media."[12] The witty Schieber has worked closely with fellow privatization advocate William Shipman, a Boston investor and former executive at State Street Bank who cochairs the Cato privatization project with Piñera.

In 1997, Piñera accompanied Ed Crane on a visit to the Governor's Mansion in Austin, Texas, where they had been invited to dine with Governor

George W. Bush and discuss their favorite subject. According to Crane, Bush told them that privatization is "the most important policy issue facing the United States today."[13] No doubt he was impressed by the prevailing Cato wisdom of the time, which predicted that Social Security would be "bankrupt" by 2006.

When he declared his candidacy for president, Bush briefly noted his interest in private accounts. He mentioned it occasionally during the 2000 campaign, most memorably when he mocked his Democratic opponents because "they want the federal government controlling the Social Security like it's some kind of federal program."[14]

Bush managed to strike a more coherent theme when he claimed the system faced fiscal problems that could only be solved if we "trust younger workers to manage some of their own money." Unless the system included some form of privatization, he warned that "it's going to be impossible to bridge the gap without causing huge payroll taxes or major benefit reductions."[15] At the same time, he vowed to protect the Social Security Trust Fund from the wastrels in Washington, D.C.

"In my economic plan, more than $2 trillion of the federal surplus is locked away for Social Security," he said in Rancho Cucamonga, California, on May 15, 2000. "For years, politicians have dipped into the trust fund to pay for more spending. And I will stop it."[16]

Pressed for details about privatizing the system, Bush always demurred, provoking Democratic nominee Al Gore to accuse him of concealing a "secret" and "risky" scheme. The Republicans denied that charge, and Gore was pilloried for exaggerating the danger. (Four years later the Democrat turned out to be more right than wrong.)

On Election Day 2000, Bush lost the popular ballot by more than three million votes to Gore and Ralph Nader. That moral defeat of Bush's conservatism can be attributed in part to public concern over his threat to Social Security. Polling data showed powerful support for the system across all age groups and strong opposition to privatization.[17] Gore's proposals to protect Social Security were far more popular than Bush's vague ideas.

Yet with the help of five Supreme Court justices, including one appointed by his father, Bush elbowed his way past Gore into the Oval Office. The new president's appointments reflected his own long-standing zeal to phase out Social Security in the name of "reform." Treasury Secretary Paul O'Neill spoke openly of his disdain for Social Security and Medicare. The same was true of Lawrence Lindsey, the Feldstein acolyte chosen to head the National Economic Council.

Lindsey devised a plan to fund the transition cost of privatization by borrowing trillions of dollars. The federal government would eventually repay those borrowed funds by capturing a portion of the high returns earned by people who had opted for private accounts. The numbers for Lindsey's "free lunch" plan didn't compute, according to worried Treasury officials.[18] This casual approach to the inherent problems of changing to "personal accounts" astonished critics such as Krugman, who wondered what the privatizers had been doing for the past quarter-century as they awaited this opportunity. It was amazing that they had developed no plausible answers to the obvious questions provoked by their scheme.

Actually, neither Bush nor most members of his team worried much about the real costs of privatization. After all, these were the "fiscal conservatives" whose first priority was a series of tax cuts that would ruin the nation's hard-earned fiscal balance and ensure huge deficits for decades to come.

Far from protecting the Clinton surplus or defending the Social Security "lockbox," Bush immediately spent the former on tax cuts and raided the latter to finance his deficits. (Economist Max Sawicky estimated in April 2005 that the Bush administration had borrowed almost $640 billion from the trust fund during its first four years in office.)[19] Bush's squandering of the surplus and ravaging of future tax revenues were the primary threat to the future solvency of Social Security and the government's capacity to redeem the bonds held by the trust fund.

In essence, Bush planned to mortgage the retirement security of the vast majority of Americans to pay for tax cuts enjoyed by a tiny, very wealthy minority. And if he could, he would burden future taxpayers with an extra few trillion in debt to pay for his privatization scheme. Explained honestly, that kind of plan would provoke public outrage.

But the Bush White House had mastered the art of rhetorical camouflage. The same public relations matrix used by Karl Rove to sell "compassionate conservatism" and fashion a new image for the Republican Party would inspire the naming of the president's Commission to Strengthen Social Security.

The cochairs of the Bush commission were Richard Parsons, the chief operating officer of Time Warner, an African American and prominent Republican, and Daniel Patrick Moynihan, the New York Democrat who had just retired after a quarter-century of service in the United States Senate. Along with Parsons and Moynihan, Bush named fourteen additional members, of whom equal numbers were said to be Republicans and Democrats—in theory, at least, a bipartisan group.

The Republicans named to the commission included Gerald Parsky, an investment manager with close ties to Karl Rove who served as California chairman of Bush–Cheney 2000; John Cogan, a former Reagan administration official and fellow at the conservative Hoover Institution, who had advised Bush on Social Security issues during the 2000 campaign; Gwendolyn S. King, who had served as a Social Security Administration commissioner during

## The President's Commission to Privatize Social Security

Karl Rove, chief political adviser to President Bush, speaks as Reverend Jerry Falwell listens during commencement at Falwell's Liberty University on May 8, 2004, in Lynchburg, Virginia. Rove, who received an honorary doctorate in the humanities, told graduates to have the courage to "do what's right, regardless of consequence, fashion or fad." (© *Eric Brady/Getty Images*)

the first Bush administration; Thomas R. Saving, a Texas economist and privatization advocate appointed by Bush as a public trustee of the Social Security and Medicare systems; Robert G. De Posada, executive director of the Hispanic Business Roundtable; and Leanne Abdnor, a former Cato Institute vice president who, at the behest of the National Association of Manufacturers, had organized a privatization lobby misleadingly named the Alliance for Worker Retirement Security.

As for the Democrats, Moynihan had joined with his colleague, Nebraska Democrat Bob Kerrey, in 1998 to propose a complex scheme that would have sharply reduced future Social Security benefits in order to finance private accounts for younger workers. (It would also have raised the retirement age and increased the income cap on the payroll tax every year as wages increased.) A lifelong supporter of the Social Security system, Moynihan resented anyone calling this plan a form of "privatization," but that is certainly what it was—and as such won almost no support from other elected Democrats.

The other commission members included in the Democratic column were Tim Penny, a former Minnesota congressman; Sam Beard, a foundation executive who had once worked for Robert F. Kennedy; Estelle James, a consultant to the World Bank; Robert Pozen, the vice chairman of Fidelity Investments; Robert Johnson, the chairman and CEO of Black Entertainment Television; and Olivia Mitchell, executive director of the Pension Research Council at the University of Pennsylvania's business school.

While all the Republicans were bona fide party donors, activists, or appointees, the Democrats—except for Moynihan—were less strongly identified with their party, to put it mildly. The partisan affiliations of James and Mitchell were tenuous. Occasionally Johnson gave money to Democrats, but by 2001 the billionaire had begun to realize that his personal economic interest was more closely aligned with the Republican White House, and he spoke up strongly in favor of Bush's plan to repeal the estate tax.

The real ringers on the Democratic side were Beard and Penny, both of whom were plucked directly from the central offices of the privatization lobby at the Cato Institute.

Penny had retired from the House of Representatives in 1994 after six terms, and then he published two books blasting his fellow Democrats (both coauthored with Major Garrett, a conservative journalist who has worked for the *Washington Times* and Fox News Channel). He also turned up as a spokesman for the Concord Coalition, a moderately conservative "nonpartisan" group headed by former Republican Treasury secretary Peter Peterson that has devoted much of its energy to cutting or eliminating Social Security. Most recently Penny had joined Cato, for which he professed great admiration, as a "fellow in fiscal policy studies."

Awarding Penny a fellowship must have been meant to display the Republican-dominated institute's bipartisan reach, but the ex-congressman was not exactly a staunch member of the opposition. So alienated was he from the party that sent him to Capitol Hill that he ran as an independent candidate for governor of Minnesota in 2002, helping to divert more than enough votes from the Democratic candidate to ensure a Republican victory.

The aptly named Beard was a foundation executive with the National Development Council, which provided advice on community development in cities and rural areas across the country. During the preceding decades he had held federal positions in both Republican and Democratic administrations—and during the Clinton years, he had grown increasingly interested in privatizing Social Security. He had written a book on the subject and created a project within the National Development Council called "Economic Security 2000" to promote privatization.

Beard may still have regarded himself as a Democrat, and he gave a few thousand dollars a year to the party's candidates, but the Republicans were financing him. For several years prior to his appointment to Bush's commission, Beard had been soliciting money from top right-wing institutional funders—including the John M. Olin Foundation, the JM Foundation, and the David H. Koch Foundation—and had been awarded at least $165,000 in grants.[20]

Those were the same foundations that had financed the Cato Institute for many years and provided special support for its multimillion-dollar Project on Social Security Privatization. Not long after the ambitious Cato project was established in 1995, Penny and Beard were asked to join its board of advisers—no doubt because as "Democrats," they could add that shiny but elusive bipartisan aura. They could be called "Cato Institute Democrats," a miniscule and isolated subset within FDR's party.

## The President's Commission to Privatize Social Security

That kind of anomaly was to be expected, however, because the commission was designed to function as a Cato-dominated Trojan horse. In addition to the three commission members associated with Cato, the commission staff was packed with ideologues from the corporate-backed think tank. To the consternation of some commission members, notably Moynihan, the staff controlled the research and drafting of options. Cato proudly reported that its own staff had handed out pro-privatization "briefing books" to the commission members.[21]

The commission spokesman was Randy Clerihue, who had been recruited directly from Cato, where he had served as director of public affairs. (Before that, Clerihue had worked as communications director of the Heritage Foundation.) The staff economist was Andrew Biggs, who had previously worked as the assistant director of Cato's Project on Social Security Privatization, where he had written dozens of polemical articles attacking Social Security. (Biggs has since been appointed by the president to serve as assistant commissioner for policy at the Social Security Administration, which has meant promoting privatization with the system's revenues and traveling with the president to "town hall" events across the country.)

Unsurprisingly, the Cato leadership hailed Bush's stacked commission—which they knew had nothing to do with "strengthening" Social Security. And the commission members largely followed the script set out for them by the Cato staffers. In both their interim report of July 2001 and their final report issued the following December, the commissioners warned that Social Security faced a crisis of insolvency and that the only viable solutions involved substantial benefit cuts combined with some form of privatization.

Yet despite all the careful rigging of the commission—with members and staff clearly committed in advance to a preordained political outcome—the whole enterprise proved to be a resounding failure. After almost twenty years of intellectual preparation by Cato and Heritage and their comrades on the right, the preapproved presidential panel could not produce agreement on a viable "reform" plan.

Instead, the commission approved a report that included three plans endorsed by different factions. And as liberal economists Dean Baker and Mark Weisbrot pointed out gleefully, "None of these plans met the criteria that the commission initially laid down for itself: balancing the program's budget over its seventy-five-year planning horizon."[22]

Even to pretend to accomplish that goal, the commission was forced to resort to accounting tricks, such as assuming that the government would issue extra-long-term bonds that wouldn't come due until sometime past the seventy-five-year horizon. Its report also assumed an unrealistically high rate of return on equities purchased for private accounts (a common subterfuge of privatization promoters) and offered false comparisons between what workers receive today under Social Security and what they might get with private accounts decades from now.

As the Treasury Department's economists learned when they analyzed Larry Lindsey's "free lunch" plan, the math didn't work for the commission, either. Having spent seven months and more than $700,000 to prove that privatization was the inevitable wave of the future, they succeeded only in demonstrating the opposite. It didn't help, either, that the stock market bubble had burst during the first quarter of 2001—and that the market had plummeted still deeper after September 11.

Facing midterm elections and contemplating war on Iraq, the Bush administration shelved its Social Security plans. Congressional Republicans running for reelection pretended that they had never supported any scheme to undermine the nation's social insurance system.

The very term *privatization* suddenly went out of fashion. The Cato Institute's Project on Social Security Privatization was abruptly transformed into the "Project on Social Security Choice." Such cosmetic changes made little difference during an election year in which disappointing stock prices were driven down still further by the cratering of the Enron Corporation, the greatest corporate scandal in decades.

In that infamous bust-out were multiple ironies for the would-be privatizers. Enron and its chairman

Kenneth Lay had been generous donors to Cato and vocal proponents of the privatization of everything everywhere. And, of course, the notion that a nation of investors would be eager to turn Social Security over to Wall Street had made perfect sense—until those horrified investors saw how much value their investments had lost in a single year.

The Cato Institute and Wall Street would have to wait until after the next election to resume the push for privatization. In the meantime, they would seek to create the facsimile of a grassroots movement supporting privatization—or what the political consulting industry calls "Astroturf."

# 3

# Under the Astroturf Carpet

On a weekday morning in July 2004, a chance mishap led to a brief, unscripted encounter on cable television that revealed how modern conservatism seeks to manufacture the appearance of broad public support for its agenda.

Viewers of C-SPAN's *Washington Journal*, the early-morning interview program on the cable network that broadcasts proceedings of the House and the Senate, were expecting to see an interview with a black conservative. Mychal Massie, a retired businessman affiliated with a right-wing African American organization known as Project 21, was scheduled to appear at 9:30 A.M. EST.

His mission, speaking on behalf of Project 21 and black conservatives in general, was to denounce the "liberalism" and other sins of the National Association for the Advancement of Colored People (NAACP), America's largest and oldest civil rights organization. He intended to refute certain derogatory remarks recently uttered by NAACP chairman Kweisi Mfume, who had mocked black conservatives as mercenaries and hustlers with no significant base in their own community.

Massie never arrived at the C-SPAN studio on Capitol Hill, however, because his car got a flat tire. Someone else from Project 21 had to rush over to take his place in front of the camera. Nobody was available on such short notice except the group's executive director.

This sudden change clearly stunned Robb Harlston, the C-SPAN anchor hosting *Washington Journal* that morning, who also happens to be black. Staring at the man who had walked into the studio and introduced himself as Project 21's executive director, Harlston couldn't help blurting the obvious on live television. "Um . . . Project 21 . . . a program for conservative African-Americans. . . . You're not African-American."[1]

Harlston was quite right: David Almasi, the executive director and sole employee of a group purporting to speak for African Americans, was undeniably a white man.

Joshua Holland, a writer for *The Gadflyer* who watched this spectacle unfold on his television screen, aptly described Almasi's surprise appearance as "an awkward Wizard of Oz moment."[2] It laid bare the real relationship between what appeared to be a black grassroots organization and its sponsors in the Republican political apparatus.

Almasi, whose résumé describes him as a "public relations veteran" with experience at several conservative outfits in Washington, quickly tried to explain away his embarrassing whiteness. "I want to make clear right at the beginning that I'm an employee, I'm an employee of Project 21, my bosses are the [black] members of Project 21, the volunteers. . . . I take my marching orders from them, not from anybody else."

Actually, Almasi takes his marching orders and his paycheck from his real bosses at the National Center for Public Policy Research (NCPPR), a Washington-based right-wing think tank and direct-mail outfit that created Project 21 as an "initiative" more than a decade ago. The aim was to put black faces on conservative messages—through an entity operated and funded by white conservatives.

Although neither as large nor as well known as Heritage and Cato, the NCPPR is very well connected in Washington Republican circles. Until October 2004, the group's board included Jack Abramoff, the supremely powerful lobbyist and Republican activist currently under investigation by the Justice Department and the Senate Commerce Committee for swindling Indian tribes and corrupting members of Congress.

According to Senate investigators, Abramoff used NCPPR to funnel at least $2.5 million in "charitable donations" from his clients to other entities that the lobbyist controlled. Abramoff also used the conservative group as a front to set up a lavish trip to Britain—including a golf vacation at St. Andrews—for House Majority Leader Tom DeLay, his wife, and two other members of Congress. NCPPR president

Amy Moritz Ridenour has said that her organization is cooperating with the investigations of Abramoff and his cronies.[3]

Money from dubious lobbyists alone hasn't kept NCPPR afloat. Like Cato and Heritage, the smaller think tank has received a stream of annual subsidies for decades from the Scaife, Castle Rock (Coors), and Bradley Foundations that total well into the millions of dollars. But the NCPPR has raised additional millions by using methods that demonstrate a special contempt not only for Social Security but for the retired Americans who depend on it.

To finance the center's privatization project—known as the "National Retirement Security Task Force"—Ridenour has relied for years on direct-mail solicitations to senior citizens that feature screaming headlines and frightening text telling them that their Social Security benefits are in imminent danger—and that to forestall disaster they must send a donation right away.

Arriving in official-looking envelopes, these letters featured shrieking bold headlines:

**A SOCIAL SECURITY CRISIS IS UPON US. SOCIAL SECURITY IS GOING BANKRUPT. . . .**

Written by direct-mail professionals and signed by Ridenour, they warned:

> The liberal monster is primed to rip your
> Social Security to shreds. . . . Inside your sealed
> envelope is information regarding the potential
> collapse of the Social Security system—and
> how it can endanger you and the entire United
> States senior citizen population. . . . It is also
> critical that you share this pertinent informa-
> tion **ONLY** with other trustworthy individuals.

In other words, don't show it to your children or
your nurse, lest they drop it in the trash.

"Should we put most of our time and effort into
fighting to prevent liberal big-spenders from drain-
ing an estimated $100 billion from the trust fund?"
a Ridenour letter would ask. "Or should I go head
to head against the left-wing's reckless use of $70
billion tax surplus when they promised to put our
Social Security first?" Invariably her terrifying message would conclude with a heartfelt pitch. "I only
hope that I am not too late. All I have is my faith that
you will trust me enough to send your vital $75 today."

In a 1998 investigation of abusive direct-mail
marketing by political hucksters, the *San Francisco
Chronicle* reported that the NCPPR regularly sent
hundreds of letters a year to the same lists of elderly
"suckers." The Social Security Administration has
long worried that such letters manipulate recipients
by convincing them that their benefits could be cut
off if they don't reply to "fright mail" with contributions. To Ridenour, these unethical tactics were

merely business as usual. "It's just that you're competing with a lot of other organizations," she said. "People seem to respond better to emotion than they do with letters that have lots and lots of facts."[4]

The alarmist tone of Ridenour's letters polluted her think tank's more serious publications as well. Indeed, the money sent in by her aging donors has been used to disseminate many rather shaky "facts." Back in 1998, for instance, the NCPPR published a pro-privatization essay quoting the Cato Institute to suggest that "Social Security will be bankrupt by 2012, possibly even by 2006."[5] In keeping with the style of Cato and Heritage, NCPPR "studies" invariably exaggerated the potential returns from private accounts, while omitting mention of the staggering costs.

Such persistent distortions are necessary to the privatization cause, but not sufficient to achieve its aims. Sophisticated conservatives have long understood that they can never succeed in dismantling Social Security—or achieving their other long-term objectives—if the only visible and enthusiastic supporters of their policies are wealthy white men. That is why they have spent millions of dollars to construct and promote organizations like Project 21 that seem to speak for more popular constituencies, including women, senior citizens, young people, and minorities.

Not all of these efforts deserve to be derided as pure "Astroturf," the term used to describe patently phony "grassroots" groups engineered by political consultants and direct-mail companies. Obviously there are sincere conservatives who happen to be black, Hispanic, female, young, and old. Yet often these organizations have no organic existence, no substantial membership, and thus little independence from their backers. (Project 21, for example, claims to have about four hundred members, although it appears that only a couple dozen are active. The membership of the NAACP is estimated at more than half a million.) The least legitimate among them usually share certain characteristics, which include overlapping personnel and total reliance on the largesse of conservative foundations and corporations.

Within modern conservatism, these constituency-oriented organizations fulfill various purposes, from recruiting fresh faces to deflecting charges of racism to attacking established civil rights and advocacy organizations. A right-wing black minister such as Project 21 member (and publicity hound) Reverend Jesse Lee Peterson sounds more credible than a white conservative when he appears on Fox News Channel to complain that by protecting Social Security, "the Democratic Party is working to keep black folks on the plantation of the government."[6]

Nothing could be more useful to the privatization campaign than erecting that kind of populist facade.

## THE RAW DEAL

African Americans play a special role in the game of symbolic politics. Their historical ordeal has endowed them with a degree of moral authority possessed by no other American ethnic group, which they brought to the New Deal coalition and the Democratic Party. For the would-be privatizers, therefore, black Americans represent an important constituency to be pulled away from that historic coalition if it is to be defeated on the quintessential issue of Social Security.

Convincing black Americans that Social Security is a "bad deal" for them and their families has been a key element of the overall privatization strategy for more than two decades. Conservatives have claimed that Social Security "discriminates" against blacks and other minorities since 1983, when the National Center for Policy Analysis—yet another right-wing think tank, based in Dallas, Texas—issued a study claiming that the average young black male wouldn't live long enough to collect retirement benefits.[7] According to the center's website, its findings "appeared on the front page of countless newspapers across the country."

Playing the race card has remained a favorite gambit of the privatization lobby, with Project 21 and other conservative groups disgorging piles of reports, studies, press releases, and op-ed columns over the past ten years devoted to the same general theme that Social Security is unfair to black Americans.

## Under the Astroturf Carpet

In 1998, the Heritage Foundation released a pair of extensive studies that addressed how the nation's two largest minority populations, African Americans and Hispanics, fare under Social Security.[8] Predictably, both studies suggested that the system is a swindle for minority workers, who would be better off with private accounts (and both studies were widely publicized in the mainstream and right-wing media).

That the Heritage ideologues were hypocritical in exploiting a race-based appeal—when they otherwise insist that public policy must be "colorblind"—may be too obvious to require discussion. On this issue, however, hypocrisy was the least of their offenses.

Not long after the Heritage studies on black and Hispanic "rates of return" appeared, authoritative government analysts blew them away for employing false assumptions, erroneous calculations and flawed methodology. So gross were these mistakes that it was difficult to determine whether they were evidence of deception or astonishing incompetence—except that they all tended to bias the studies in favor of privatization.

For instance, the Heritage studies failed to account for survivor and disability benefits, which are paid disproportionately to black families. Nonpartisan researchers have found that Social Security benefits play an important role in keeping blacks above the poverty level, both in retirement and when black workers die or become disabled.

The Social Security Administration's Office of the Chief Actuary—widely respected among economists and statisticians of all political persuasions—disparaged the Heritage conclusions about African Americans as "highly misleading due to two major errors in methodology, plus a number of incorrect or inappropriate assumptions."[9] Those bogus methods led Heritage to find "differences in rates of return by race that are greatly exaggerated."[10] Many of the same errors turned up in the study of Hispanics—and the actuary's office also noted that the Heritage analysts neglected to mention that Hispanics "would be expected to receive a substantially higher rate of return from Social Security than would the general population"[11] because they tend to live longer than average.

The Government Accountability Office (GAO), which conducts audits and investigations for Congress, likewise dismissed the Heritage findings. Testifying before the House subcommittee on Social Security in February 1999, a GAO analyst patiently explained that the Heritage study was misleading because it focused on African American life expectancy without accounting for other factors that affect benefit levels.

"Social Security's progressive benefit formula has particular importance for blacks and Hispanics because they tend to have lower lifetime taxable earnings than whites," said Cynthia Fagnoni, the agency's director of income security studies. The progressive benefit formula used to determine Social Security benefits, she added, erases any negative effect caused by African Americans' lower life expectancy.[12]

Among the other substantial deceptions in both Heritage studies was the omission of certain highly relevant facts about private accounts. Such tricks, which are typical of privatization propaganda aimed at whites as well as minorities, include ignoring the administrative costs of individual accounts, the annual fees charged by investment firms and mutual funds, and the price of converting such accounts to annuities upon retirement. Those charges can consume 30 percent or more of total earnings—and they are applied regardless of race or ethnicity.[13]

Four years later, in 2003, the GAO issued a new report that again found no discrimination against blacks in the distribution of Social Security benefits.[14] In fact, competent researchers have repeatedly proved that social insurance protects families of all races from poverty.

Yet President Bush and his allies were scarcely discouraged by such well-established facts from pursuing their demagogic racial strategy. Their campaign for private accounts quickly revived the discredited Heritage studies—and bolstered them with presidential prestige. On January 24, 2005, Bush held a closed meeting at the White House with about twenty prominent black conservatives associated with Cato, Heritage, Project 21, and other groups—mostly clergymen, business executives and lawyers—who served as convenient props to deliver his message. "African-American males die sooner than other males do," according to the president, "which means the system is inherently unfair to a certain group of people."[15]

So far, black Americans seem skeptical about these expressions of concern from the president and other conservatives, who are not known for excessive worrying about U.S. society's mistreatment of minorities. Some black leaders ask why the president isn't doing more to reduce racial differences in life span, income, and medical care, rather than merely citing them for partisan advantage. Recent polls show that black voters have rejected Bush's Social Security plan even more decisively than the rest of their fellow citizens.[16]

While conservatives may well have hoped to persuade minorities to support privatization, the value of that effort has always been more symbolic than practical. The right appears to have recognized the inherent difficulty of organizing blacks and Hispanics against Social Security, which has proved so beneficial to their communities for so many years. A few black conservatives have been mobilized behind privatization through Project 21—which already existed to oppose affirmative action and advance broader conservative goals—but there are no privatization groups within minority communities.

## Under the Astroturf Carpet

Meanwhile, however, organizations of varying sizes and descriptions have emerged to sell privatization to a skeptical public. Some of these groups appear to exist only as propagandistic websites with no identifiable leadership, such as the strange Retiresafe.org; others feature the same few names associated with the Cato Institute and the President's Commission to Strengthen Social Security; still others seem to function strictly as tentacles of White House deputy chief of staff (and unofficial GOP boss) Karl Rove. In keeping with the "message discipline" of the Bush White House and the conservative movement, they coordinate constantly and repeat the same phrases about "strengthening Social Security" with "personal accounts."

So many of these organizations have cropped up, in fact, that the privatization lobby has come to resemble a conglomerate metastasizing out of control. Aside from the traditional array of major right-wing edifices—including Cato, Heritage, the American Enterprise Institute, Americans for Tax Reform, the National Center for Policy Analysis, the National Center for Public Policy Research, the Hoover Institution, and the Manhattan Institute—the privatization coalition includes a number of additional entities of varying authenticity.

Perhaps the most "real" is the awkwardly named FreedomWorks, a national membership organization with chapters in several states and funding from the Koch brothers as well as various corporations and foundations. FreedomWorks was known as Citizens for a Sound Economy until July 2004, when it merged with Empower America, a conservative activist group founded by William Bennett and former representative Jack Kemp. The combined organization, which claims more than 350,000 members, is cochaired by Kemp, former House majority leader Dick Armey and C. Boyden Gray, a Washington lawyer with close ties to the Bush White House. With various arms that permit FreedomWorks to engage in partisan politics, it mobilized in 2004 on behalf of the Bush–Cheney campaign and Republican candidates in battleground states. Since the election, privatization has been its top priority.

Other than FreedomWorks, most of the other groups in the privatization network exist as little more than letterheads and websites. To understand the lobby's motives and strategies, it is instructive to examine such pure Astroturf entities as For Our Grandchildren, RetireSafe.org, and Women for a Social Security Choice. The latter was set up by Leanne Abdnor, a veteran corporate lobbyist and Republican activist, who has declined to reveal the sources of its funding. It has no members.

Abdnor herself is virtually a human template of the privatization network. Back in the Nixon era, she began her Washington career as an assistant to Senator Strom Thurmond. She became a lobbyist and eventually was hired to represent Koch Industries—founding corporate patron of the Cato Institute and FreedomWorks—on Capitol Hill.

Ten years ago, Abdnor joined Cato as the think tank's "vice president of external affairs" and, working with Jose Piñera, became a fervent exponent of Social Security privatization. (She happens to be trained as a schoolteacher, not an economist.) She is currently the executive director of Women for a Social Security Choice and serves on the national advisory council of For Our Grandchildren—still another Astroturf outfit that appears to have been set up as a mouthpiece for the members of the Bush commission, since most of them are also on its board.

How all these overlapping organizations fit together became clearer in a story that appeared in December 2004 in the *New York Times*, during the president's national tour of "town hall" meetings to promote privatization. Tightly controlled, with entry permitted only to fervent supporters, those events featured "regular folks" interacting with Bush to discuss the impending "bankruptcy" of Social Security and the wondrous benefits of private accounts. Naturally, such a show looks more convincing if the cast of characters is diverse enough to include women, blacks, and young people.

So when the White House needed a presentable woman to chat with the president about the private account she hoped to someday leave to her little daughter, the perfect candidate was Sandy Jacques of Iowa. Here was somebody who could speak for the soccer moms of America. Why would anyone need to know that, as the *Times* reported, Jacques happens to be the Iowa state director of Freedom-Works, the Iowa spokeswoman of For Our Grand-children—and also (as the *Times* didn't mention) a member of the advisory board of Women for a Social Security Choice?[17]

Although Abdnor has told reporters that her group is "independent of the White House," she worked as a supporting act for several of Bush's town meetings, appearing with him in Florida, Colorado, and Arizona. Her busy schedule over the past year has also taken her to editorial boards, television and radio interviews, and public appearances across the country. Her former boss at Cato, Ed Crane, proudly calls her "a leader of the movement."[18]

In a sense, outfits like Project 21 and Women for a Social Security Choice don't need to succeed in any conventional sense. By manufacturing the appearance of diversity, they have achieved as much as their creators could reasonably expect. For conservatives, courting women and minorities is an unavoidable if often unrewarding political necessity.

The privatization network's most important propaganda targets are based not on race or gender but on age. In their 1983 "Leninist" blueprint, Stuart Butler and Peter Germanis emphasized outreach to the young, who might be enticed by promised returns from private accounts, and to the old, whose political power had to be "neutralized" before Congress would legislate privatization. Butler and Germanis believed that "the young are the most obvious constituency for reform and a natural ally of the private alternative."[19]

The most ambitious attempt to mobilize young Americans in favor of privatization began in 1993 with the founding of a new Generation X group called Third Millennium. Among its early leaders were Jonathan Karl, a former campus conservative who went on to become a White House correspondent for CNN; Douglas Kennedy, a son of the late Robert F. Kennedy who became a reporter for Fox News Channel; and Deroy Murdock, a black conservative who became a syndicated newspaper columnist (and a member of Project 21).

Third Millennium reached its zenith in late 1994, as the Republicans were taking over Congress, when it released a national survey of young adults and senior citizens concerning their attitudes toward Social Security. Conducted jointly by Republican Frank Luntz and a Democratic consultant named Mark Siegel, the poll "found that more Americans ages 18–34 believe UFOs exist (46 percent) than believe Social Security will exist by the time they retire (28 percent)." According to Third Millennium cofounder Richard Thau, this "factoid" quickly became "one of the most often-cited poll statistics of the 1990s." Thau credited conservative columnist Murdock with the idea of comparing Social Security to an unidentified flying object, which represented alleged resentment among young workers over paying taxes "into a system that we don't think will be there for us."[20]

But although the UFO factoid got wide publicity—and probably helped to undermine support for Social Security among young Americans—Third Millennium never grew into a viable organization. Lacking political appeal, it was eventually eclipsed by Rock the Vote, which focused on voter registration but has since taken up the defense of Social Security against privatization.

When Bush announced the formation of his Commission to Strengthen Social Security in 2001, Third Millennium was already on the wane. While Thau was invited to the official announcement at the White House, neither he nor anyone from his group was asked to sit on the commission. "I got a moment to thank the President for trying to reform Social Security for Americans in their twenties and thirties," he recalled. "It was an honor to be in the Rose Garden for the event."[21] Two years later, Third Millennium stopped updating its website and closed its doors. Whatever doubts young people may feel about Social Security, they have displayed little interest in organizing to phase out the system. That effort has been taken up by the College Republicans, the organization that nurtured Karl Rove and Grover Norquist.

If the young lack enthusiasm for privatization, the elderly continue to stand as a staunch and perhaps immovable bloc in opposition. With more than thirty-five million members, the AARP has proved to be the single most daunting obstacle confronted by the Bush White House and its allies. Nonpartisan and service oriented, with hundreds of millions of dollars earned annually from membership dues and sales of prescription drugs, travel packages, credit cards, and insurance plans, the AARP has long been among the most powerful lobbying organizations in Washington.

AARP's determination to thwart privatization could not be any clearer than in a letter to members posted on its website by its president Marie Smith and CEO Bill Novelli. This pithy declaration describes the essential elements of any plan to ensure the retirement system's future solvency: a "risk-free" retirement benefit that can't be outlived; disability and survivor benefits for workers and their families; a minimum level of decent benefits for low-wage retirees; and benefits that are based on contributions, plus annual cost-of-living adjustments. In short, the AARP expects Social Security to continue as a progressive social insurance program.

To rule out any misunderstanding, Novelli and Smith went on to explain precisely what the AARP would not accept. "Private accounts that take money out of Social Security are not part of the solution," said their letter. "These accounts drain money out of Social Security, cut benefits and pass the bill to future generations. . . . We will not waver in our commitment to Social Security and will remain firm in our stance against any plan that takes money out of Social Security."[22] In other words, their policy leaves no space for compromise with the president's top domestic objective for his second term.

After suffering through two national waves of AARP-sponsored television advertising that mocked privatization as a stupid gamble, Bush was publicly pleading for mercy by March 2005. Actually, he prevailed on his former Republican rival John McCain to make the plea on his behalf, during a town hall meeting in New Mexico.

"I want to say to our friends in the AARP—and they are my friends: Come to the table with us," said the Arizona senator.[23] He might have saved his breath.

After helping the president to win passage of his costly Medicare "reform" legislation in 2003, the AARP leadership had endured an angry reaction from millions of their members who had opposed that wasteful bill and its overly complicated prescription drug benefit.

Novelli hadn't backed off, but he had felt stung by accusations of betrayal from traditional allies. He had prepared for the Social Security debate by conducting extensive polling and public discussion of the issue. He and Smith were confident that their position was strongly supported by the overwhelming majority of their membership, and subsequent surveys by news organizations indicated that they were correct.[24]

AARP nevertheless presented a large, tempting target to what might be called the "grifter" element of the Republican right. It was probably inevitable that conservatives would seek to contest the sprawling political terrain controlled by the senior citizen organization. But the hucksters who challenged AARP over privatization brought no credit on their cause or to the president.

Actually, the right-wing group known as United Seniors Association (which, as noted earlier, has started to call itself USA Next) had nagged and needled the AARP for years without attracting much attention. With the commencement of the struggle over Social Security, however, there came new opportunities for publicity.

The man who created United Seniors in 1991 was ultraright direct-mail impresario Richard Viguerie, an industry pioneer and dedicated ideologue who has wanted to abolish Social Security ever since he worked in the Goldwater campaign.[25] Under his leadership, United Seniors protected the interests of seniors about as reliably as Colonel Sanders protected the interests of chickens. He originated the direct-mail "Social Security" ploy later used by dozens of groups, notably the National Center for Public Policy Research, to separate naive senior citizens from their money.

On United Seniors letterhead, Viguerie regularly sent ominous, official-looking letters to elderly voters, telling them that politicians had "spent all

Richard Viguerie, a fund-raiser for conservative causes, poses amid computer tapes on which were stored data for fund-raising. (© Wally McNamee/CORBIS)

the money" in the Social Security trust fund. To rescue their retirement, he urged the jittery seniors to send checks immediately to his post office box. He churned out these mailings by the millions while pocketing a hefty proportion of the profits—and prompting investigations by state and federal agencies.[26]

Aside from swelling his own fortune, Viguerie's purpose was to finance conservative propaganda. He could scare old people into sending him money, and then use their donations to promote Republican cutbacks in their Medicare benefits.[27] He possessed an ironic sense of humor.

Viguerie has since moved on, but United Seniors continues under the leadership of one Charlie Jarvis, a religious-right activist and former Reagan administration official. Unlike his predecessor, who kept a low profile for decades, Jarvis enjoys press attention and sometimes talks more than he should. In a brief interview with the *New York Times Magazine*, he agreed that he saw his mission as "dismantling Social Security."[28]

United Seniors' counsel is another former Reagan official named Curtis Herge, whose previous legal clients include a phony Holocaust survivors group[29] and a bogus antigambling organization that once fronted for casino mogul Donald Trump—all of which qualified him to represent an organization that maintains the business ethic established by its founder.[30]

In August 2003, the federal government fined United Seniors more than $500,000 for sending out "misleading" mail designed to look like "some sort of official mailing containing information from the Social Security Administration."[31] (Until 2002, the directors of USA Next included the ubiquitous and highly dubious lobbyist Jack Abramoff.)

While Jarvis likes to boast that United Seniors has more than a million members, very few of them seem to pay membership dues, according to the organization's tax returns. Of more than $25 million in revenues reported for 2003, less than $2 million was attributed to membership dues. In recent years, most of its budget has been subsidized by the pharmaceutical industry, which essentially uses United Seniors to launder support to Republican members of Congress. The *Washington Monthly* reported that during the 2002 midterm elections, United Seniors spent about $14 million in "unrestricted educational grants" from drug companies on advertising "defending" GOP incumbents for voting in favor of Bush's Medicare bill.[32]

Not long after the president commenced his privatization campaign, Jarvis launched his latest blitz against the AARP. The pretext was new, but the rhetoric was familiar. United Seniors had attacked AARP many times, invariably and tiresomely accusing the bipartisan lobby of "liberalism." The only notable innovation—which attracted immediate media coverage—came when Jarvis announced that he had hired the same political consultants who produced the "Swift Boat" commercials that defamed Democrat John Kerry during the 2004 presidential campaign. These right-wing assassins, he vowed, would "dynamite" the AARP.[33]

In a demonstration of the firepower they threatened to use, Jarvis posted an ad on the website of *The American Spectator* magazine. The tiny ad insinuated that the utterly mainstream and traditional AARP disdains American soldiers and advocates gay marriage. Few AARP members were likely to believe such sensational lies, but the ad provided a momentary media impact. (It also sparked a lawsuit by the gay married couple whose wedding photo appeared in the ad without their permission.)

Such farcical assaults scarcely rose to the level of harassment, like a flea gnawing at an elephant. When Jarvis first announced his jihad against AARP, he had vowed to pull away a million members, no doubt hoping that they would enrich him and his colleagues.[34] Instead, the AARP continued to grow at an unusually rapid rate.

Still, despite its unsavory personnel and crude tactics, United Seniors was welcomed into the privatization network. The corporate interests at the heart of that network knew they could rely on Charlie Jarvis to sweep their sleazy money and their real purposes under the Astroturf carpet.

# 4

# Wall Street's Inevitable Trillion-Dollar Windfall

In the national debate over Social Security, the argument between the privatization lobby and its opponents revolves around what will happen to the U.S. economy and American society decades from now. Based on economic models used by the Congressional Budget Office, defenders of the system believe that its reserves will continue to finance full benefits until sometime between 2042 and 2052— or more than forty years from today.[1] To ensure that the system can continue to pay full benefits thereafter, they suggest that some changes in retirement ages, cost-of-living adjustments, and taxation levels may be required.[2]

All of that will depend in turn on how quickly the economy grows, how much wages rise as a percentage of the economy, and whether immigration or other factors increase the size of the labor force. Predicting those numbers with any precision is difficult, but Social Security's proponents are consistent: They believe that unless the economy grows at an extraordinarily low rate, the retirement system can survive with only minor changes over time.

The privatizers, by contrast, argue from premises that are mutually contradictory. Their shrill, incessant warning of "bankruptcy" for Social Security is derived from conservative predictions about the future growth of the U.S. economy that cut against historic trends. Their upbeat outlook on private accounts, however, is based on the rather optimistic notion that the stock market will perform as well in the future as in the past.

They seem to be telling us that the market will trend upward while the economy trends downward. You don't have to be an economist to understand that those predictions are unlikely to be true simultaneously, although many economists have pointed it out.

With such tendentious disputes among experts about the shape of things to come, it isn't surprising that those same sages are unable to agree about the potential risks and rewards of privatized accounts versus Social Security benefits. When considering the privatization argument, it's important to remember that Social Security isn't a retirement annuity or a 401k account but a guarantee of social insurance—a system in which society joins together through government to protect potentially vulnerable people from disability and the loss of a family breadwinner, as well as from poverty in old age. Otherwise the comparison between private accounts and Social Security can be misleading.

## Wall Street's Inevitable Trillion-Dollar Windfall

What can also be misleading, or at least confusing, are the widely varying prognostications about the future performance of the stock market. The reason it is illegal to offer guarantees about stocks and other investments is that nobody can honestly be certain about how well they will do. That doesn't discourage some people from pretending to such certainty. Although the privatizers are careful not to promise anything specific, the figures they toss around for stock appreciation certainly sound promising.

As might be expected, the Cato Institute houses many of privatization's most bullish advocates. Its website pumps up enthusiasm with the vague assertion that "over the last eighty years, private investment in the United States has earned an average annual return of nearly 8 percent."[3] William Shipman, a former executive with State Street Bank who has long cochaired the Cato's privatization project, says that over the past seventy-five years, the "compounded annual real rate of return" from a balanced fund of stocks and bonds came to 6.2 percent.[4] Cato vice president Michael Tanner admits that projecting future equity returns is "difficult" but says that 6.5 percent is "well within the range of reasonable estimates."[5] Andrew Biggs, the former Cato analyst who now serves as a presidential adviser on Social Security, raised the stakes by claiming that the "real return to capital . . . has averaged 8.5 percent before taxes over the last forty years."[6] Former Cato fellow Stephen Moore, who has continued to promote privatization at the Club for Growth and the Free Enterprise Fund, outbid Biggs: "Over the last sixty years stocks have provided an average annual return reaching near 10 percent."[7]

Their enthusiasm for privatization is matched by James Glassman, a syndicated columnist, American Enterprise Institute fellow, and trustee of the libertarian Reason Foundation. Glassman's endorsement of the Bush privatization scheme is underscored by his scorn for Social Security, which he denounces as "a blight on liberty" and a "Ponzi scheme" that probably should never have existed.[8]

Confident that stocks would swiftly triple in value, Glassman and a former Federal Reserve economist named Kevin Hassett coauthored a book titled *Dow 36,000: The New Strategy for Profiting from the Coming Rise in the Stock Market.* They published this ill-timed tome in September 1999, only months before the dot-com bubble deflated and stock prices began to fall. (At this writing, the Dow Jones remains well below the 11,000 mark reached around the time that Glassman and Hassett's book appeared, urging everybody to buy, buy, buy.)

Yale economist Robert Shiller has urged a more sober approach. Commenting on likely future equity returns for retirees, Shiller dismisses the overly optimistic estimates flung around by privatization proponents such as the Cato crowd and Glassman. He notes that the Bush plan to privatize Social Security relies on estimated returns of 6.5 percent, an outcome that he regards as far from probable. According to him, the likeliest return to stock ownership in coming decades is no higher than 4.6 percent.[9]

As Shiller explained in a March 2005 paper on how future equity and bond prices might affect privatized Social Security accounts, it is quite likely that the results for retirees would be disappointing. His models suggest that the returns would be impressive in very few cases—and that up to 71 percent of workers who opt for private accounts could suffer a net loss compared with the income they would have received under the traditional Social Security system.[10]

The Yale professor commands attention when he speaks because—unlike Glassman, the Cato crowd, and the rest of the bullish bullshitters—he anticipated the incipient market plunge in *Irrational Exuberance*, his March 2000 book (published just as the dot-com bubble was imploding).[11] In fact, by then the prescient Shiller had been warning for several years that stocks were frighteningly overpriced.

He is hardly alone among leading financial thinkers in his skepticism about substituting private accounts for Social Security.

Sharing similar doubts are Warren Buffett and Charles Munger, the chairman and vice chairman of Berkshire Hathaway Corp., who may be the most successful investors of the past century. At their company's 2005 annual meeting, both executives told shareholders that they vehemently oppose the Bush privatization scheme. Munger, who has described himself as a "right-wing Republican," put it plainly. "The Republicans are out of their cotton-picking minds on this issue," he said, because Social Security is "one of the most successful things that the government has ever done."[12]

Within the economics profession as a whole, however, opinion is divided, mainly along ideological lines. While most liberal and centrist economists oppose the Bush scheme and privatization generally, conservative economists tend to strongly favor both. Nobel laureates can be found on either side of the debate.

Yet although economists differ over whether to privatize Social Security and how that would affect ordinary Americans, they agree broadly about one thing: Privatization would create a bonanza for the financial industry, with as many as 130 million new investment accounts that would be worth hundreds of billions of dollars. Since privatization proponents like to discuss the long term, invoking "infinite" horizons to prove that the system will become insolvent someday, it seems fair to mention that investment firms could expect to reap nearly a trillion dollars in profit from privatized Social Security accounts over the next several decades.

That is the estimate of Austan Goolsbee, a liberal University of Chicago economist who released the findings of a study he prepared during the 2004 presidential campaign. By his calculations, if annual management fees on all privatized Social Security accounts over $5,000 were set at 0.8 percent, the total fees over the seventy-five-year time horizon would come to $940 billion.[13] His estimate of fees seems conservative, considering that the average fee charged by a mutual fund today is closer to 1.09 percent. Although the Cato Institute's estimates use a considerably lower fee of 0.65 percent—or about 60 percent of the actual current level—its analyst Michael Tanner accepted Goolsbee's data. Under privatization, the Cato official conceded, a huge windfall for Wall Street would be "inevitable."[14]

Inevitable or not, that windfall would be, as the Chicago economist pointed out, the greatest bonanza in U.S. financial history.[15] The prospect of siphoning enormous fees and commissions from the Social Security revenue stream explains why Wall Street firms, investment banks, insurance companies, and stock brokerages have invested millions of dollars in the privatization campaign—through Cato, the Club for Growth, and a myriad of other think tanks and front groups.

There is nothing surprising about such hunger among financiers for the easy money privatization would deliver. Back in 1983, the "Leninist" strategy devised by Stuart Butler and Peter Germanis anticipated that corporations and financial companies would play a central role in the campaign to abolish Social Security:

> What we must do is construct a coalition . . .
> that will benefit directly from [privatization's]
> implementation. That coalition should consist
> not only of those who will reap benefits from
> the . . . private system . . . but also the banks,
> insurance companies, and other institutions
> that will gain from providing such plans to
> the public. . . .
>
> The business community, and financial
> institutions in particular, would be an obvious
> element in the constituency. Not only does
> business have a great deal to gain from a reform
> effort designed to stimulate private savings,
> but it also has the power to be politically influ-
> ential and to be instrumental in mounting a
> public education campaign.[16]

The character of this "public education" campaign can be gleaned from some of its most widely
circulated materials, such as the "calculators" set up
on the Cato and Heritage websites to ballyhoo the
enormous benefits from privatization. Both sites
offer wildly optimistic results that are based on false
assumptions about the future growth of the stock
market, the rate of wage growth, and the likely fees
and other costs assessed on private accounts. But
then, as one sympathetic blogger explained, the calculators are just "marketing tools"—in other words,
they were meant to fool ordinary citizens, not seri-

ous analysts or competent economists (or anybody who can use a real calculator).[17]

Educating the public about Social Security—as defined by business and financial interests—meant delivering an ever louder bombardment of warnings about the system's imminent "bankruptcy" and the "threat" posed by this impending disaster to the American way of life.

Among the first to yank the false alarm was Peter Peterson, an investment banker who had once served as secretary of commerce in the Nixon administration and later became chairman of Lehman Brothers, Kuhn Loeb, one of the largest investment houses on Wall Street. In December 1982, Peterson published a striking series of articles in the liberal *New York Review of Books*, in which he predicted a national economic catastrophe unless drastic cuts were made in Social Security and Medicare.

By 2005, he suggested, Social Security was likely to be running annual deficits of $100 billion a year or more.[18] The failure of gloomy prognostications to materialize has never discouraged Peterson, who founded an educational and lobbying group called the Concord Coalition to promote his views. (Since then he has also found time to cofound the Blackstone Group, an international investment giant with more than $23 billion in assets.) Over the past two decades, the Concord Coalition has received substantial donations from right-wing foundations to spread the message of gloom about Social Security, often in the form of books by Peterson.

Until the arrival of George W. Bush in the White House, however, business and financial leaders muted their hostility to Social Security, because the program was too popular to attack and also because they had other interests to pursue (in particular, tax cuts on capital gains and personal and corporate income). The first signs of a corporate campaign for privatization began to appear during the Clinton administration, fostered by the National Association of Manufacturers and the U.S. Chamber of Commerce—big business, strongly conservative, and Republican organizations that have opposed social insurance and most progressive legislation since the New Deal.

The Investment Company Institute, the Securities Industry Association, and other groups associated with the financial sector started to discuss ways to promote privatization as well. But as Tim Penny, then already working with Cato, told reporter Robert Dreyfuss in 1996, most companies were too worried about public opinion to come out boldly for privatizing Social Security. "A lot of firms are trying to find a low-key way to support this," Penny said. "I don't think you're going to see a lot of this happening under their names. They'll stay behind the scenes, twice removed."[19]

During the 1996 presidential election, as an official of NAM confided to Dreyfuss, the corporate privatizers still preferred to avoid public debate on the issue, fearing that both Clinton and his Republican opponent Bob Dole would be forced to pledge not to change the retirement system.[20] Although Clinton later flirted publicly with private-account proposals, he eventually rejected them in favor of bolstering the system by paying down national debt with surplus revenue.

Only after Bush had entered the Oval Office five years later with his retinue of right-wing economists did NAM, the Chamber of Commerce, and the financial industry revive their push for privatization. Encouraged by the White House, several significant Wall Street firms came together to push the policies to which Bush had alluded during the prior year's presidential campaign. Brought together by the Frank Russell Company (creator of the Russell 2000 stock indexes), Mellon Institutional Asset Management and State Street Global Advisors, among others, they called themselves the "Coalition for American Financial Security." In June 2001, they marked their founding with a kickoff luncheon at the Windows on the World restaurant atop the World Trade Center, with the guest of honor and main attraction sent by the White House.

"I come to you as managing trustee of Social Security," said Treasury Secretary Paul O'Neill, who had expressed his disdain for the program months earlier in an interview with the London *Financial Times*.[21] "Today we have no assets in the trust fund,"

O'Neill went on, which must have surprised anyone who read the trustees' reports he had signed, stating that the funds indeed possessed assets in the form of Treasury notes worth some $900 billion.[22] But O'Neill's political point was clear enough.

The Coalition for American Financial Security fell apart within a year after its founding, again because few of the largest investment houses were willing to commit themselves publicly to privatization. The group's disintegration was hastened when State Street Global Advisers dropped out, following the retirements of its vehemently pro-privatization chairman Marshall Carter and his associate William Shipman, who cochaired Cato's privatization project. The new management didn't want any negative publicity.

As the midterm elections approached in the fall of 2002, however, NAM and the Chamber of Commerce were busy creating a more durable lobbying group, which they dubbed the "Coalition for the Modernization and Protection of America's Social Security." Armed with $8 million to buy political advertising during the weeks leading up to Election Day, COMPASS sought to defend Republican candidates who had come under sharp attacks from the Democrats for endorsing privatization.[23] (That was when the term *privatization* suddenly went out of style on the right, to be replaced by *personal accounts*, *choice*, or *modernization*.)

In addition to NAM and the Chamber of Commerce, COMPASS counted among its supporters the American Bankers Association, the Business Roundtable (representing the CEOs of the nation's two hundred largest corporations), the National Federation of Independent Business (which lobbies on behalf of smaller companies), and the Securities Industry Association (the main Wall Street trade group and lobbying arm).[24]

Joining COMPASS and Cato at the battlefront in 2002 was the Club for Growth, a well-heeled and highly aggressive political action committee founded years earlier by conservative money managers in New York City to defeat Democrats, purge moderates from the Republican Party, and fight for lower taxes on the wealthy. Although the "club" boasts of having ten thousand members, mostly from the financial industry, the bulk of its funds are contributed by investment firms such as the giant Stephens, Inc., Strong Financial, Charles Schwab, Zweig-DiMenna Associates, Oppenheimer Capital, and Gilder Gagnon Howe & Company.[25]

Led by Stephen Moore, a former Republican congressional aide who ran the club from 1998 to 2004, it adopted Social Security privatization as a top priority. Moore not only despises Democrats but particularly dislikes Republicans of the centrist Eisenhower tradition —that is, Republicans who see any need for an economic safety net or any public provision for the elderly and the poor. Moore's views reflect the antigovernment extremism of the Cato Institute, which is hardly surprising since he is also a former Cato analyst. He is but one of many conservative apparatchiks who have passed through the revolving doors that connect Cato, the Club for Growth, COMPASS, and the Bush White House.

Among the subsidiaries of COMPASS is still another privatization front called the Alliance for Worker Retirement Security (AWRS). The founding director of AWRS was Leanne Abdnor, the former Cato official who, as noted earlier, served on Bush's Social Security commission and currently leads such Astroturf outfits as Women for Social Security Choice and For Our Grandchildren. When Abdnor left AWRS, her replacement was Charles Blahous III, who served as the executive director of the Bush commission. Since then Blahous has moved on to oversee Social Security policy in the White House, along with former Cato analyst Andrew Biggs (who also served on the staff of the Bush commission). And when Chuck Blahous left AWRS for the White House, his replacement was Derrick Max, who had worked for both NAM and Cato as a lobbyist. Max currently directs both COMPASS and AWRS.

This welter of fronts and personalities may seem bewildering, but the names of the lobbyists, spokespersons, fronts, and consultants matter less than their connections. There is no "vast right-wing conspiracy" to phase out Social Security—but there is a powerful network, backed by the largest business and financial organizations in the country, which has taken on that mission.

In 2002, COMPASS, Cato and the Club for Growth fought hard on behalf of their favorite congressional and Senate candidates, who had endorsed private accounts, but the declining stock market and the Enron scandal shut down discussion of privatization for another two years. The next great opportunity for conservatives and their corporate allies arose when Bush was reelected with a Republican majority in both the House of Representatives and the Senate.

Within weeks after the November 2004 victory, word began to leak from the White House that Social Security privatization would be the top domestic priority for the president's second term. He was prepared to take the risks inherent in achieving the goal that had eluded conservatives for decades: the elimination of the most successful and symbolic program of the New Deal and the most important legacy of the Democratic Party. Without having enunciated even the most basic elements of his privatization scheme, he also expected his allies in the business community, who had given tens of millions of dollars to his presidential campaign, to line up behind him again.

The assumption that Wall Street's giants would join Bush to win the prize of privatization didn't seem far-fetched to the financial journalist and money manager James Cramer. In a January 2005 *New York* magazine column, Cramer predicted that the president would

> ram Social Security "reform" through Congress by getting brokerage houses to lobby for the change. George Bush will promise Goldman Sachs, Morgan Stanley, Schwab, Lehman Brothers, and Bear Stearns the contract to privatize Social Security and let them be the administrators of the project. These firms will then get their employees to give millions to politicians who are on the fence. Their stocks will triple in value from the prospect of the new business, they'll pressure the Republican-led Congress for swift passage in the fall of 2005, and the deal will get done.[26]

While Cramer's scenario of legalized graft was oversimplified, he identified a critical element of the campaign for privatization that commenced with Bush's second inauguration. Yet he neglected to mention the figure who would mastermind that campaign for the White House and Wall Street: Karl Rove.

By late February 2005, Rove was marshalling not only Wall Street but Washington's entire business lobbying community behind the president's privatization plan (although at that point, there still was no specific plan endorsed by Bush). Stephen

Moore told a reporter for Bloomberg News that Rove was personally directing the campaign because "the White House feels it can't afford to lose on this. . . . There are regular meetings the White House has with all the groups to make sure everyone is singing from the same hymnal."[27] And that was certainly the signal Rove sent to his party's allies.

At a White House meeting with the leaders of dozens of trade and industry associations and lobbyists, the Republican political boss demanded that they join and support COMPASS. It was clear that "Turd Blossom," as the president affectionately calls Rove, would be taking names and kicking butts. One of the major lobbyists present at the meeting was Dirk Van Dongen, the president of the National Association of Wholesaler-Distributors and a committed Republican activist. Van Dongen later said that the White House meeting with Rove had proved that the president was "serious" about winning privatization—"and that anything business can do to help on this journey will be important. And it will be noted."[28]

In other words, even business groups that had no direct stake in privatizing Social Security were expected to support the campaign if they wanted their own interests to be advanced by the White House.

Within a few weeks after the meeting called by Rove, COMPASS announced that more than a hundred trade groups had signed up (and paid hefty annual membership fees, which topped out at $60,000). Derrick Max told reporters that COMPASS and AWRS would spend no less than $20 million on nationwide television advertising, "grassroots lobbying," and direct-mail communications to pressure Congress.[29] They suggested quietly that they might eventually spend much more than that amount.[30]

At the same time, USA Next, the senior citizens Astroturf outfit operated by Charlie Jarvis, vowed to spend up to $10 million attacking AARP. To slime the retiree group, Jarvis hired Chris LaCivita, a Republican public relations and advertising consultant known for the false and vicious campaign he had overseen during the 2004 campaign for the Swift Boat Veterans for Truth. Progress for America, a political committee set up by Bush administration donors and allies to push for his policies, likewise pledged to spend $20 million or more on television commercials attacking Democrats for "doing nothing" on Social Security and touting the president's plan to "save" the system.[31]

Messages and targeting for these organizations were coordinated with an election-style campaign operation run by the Republican National Committee (RNC). At regular meetings in the GOP headquarters, usually held on Friday afternoons, RNC staffers would sit down with officials from COMPASS and the White House Office of Public Liaison to evaluate their work and plan for the coming weeks.[32] Unlike an election campaign, when federal laws prohibit independent groups from working with the parties and candidates, there was nothing illegal about the intensive coordination between the White House and the business-backed privatization front groups.

Their methods were first tested during last winter's February recess, when members of Congress went home with instructions to promote the president's Social Security agenda. According to an internal RNC memo obtained by the *Chicago Tribune*, COMPASS staffers made more than 250,000 telephone contacts in eleven targeted districts, participated in forty-one interviews with local media, placed two hundred calls to talk radio shows, "mobilized" 3,100 advocates to attend town hall meetings with members of Congress, and placed essays by COMPASS director Derrick Max and former Oklahoma representative J. C. Watts in the newspapers of ten "local markets."[33]

Impressive as those numbers may seem, the Rove team could not have been satisfied with the results of their February blitz, when Republican politicians returned to Washington shaken by the angry reception they had found back in their districts. What the triumphant Rove may not have expected was the unified resistance against his privatization campaign—which must have been especially surprising after the grim defeat he had inflicted on his opponents only a few months earlier.

Yet those undeniably depressed Democrats and progressives showed startling vigor as they rallied to defend Social Security and the New Deal. Democratic senators and members of Congress have held surprisingly firm on Social Security, particularly when compared with earlier retreats on regressive tax cuts. The labor movement, long weakened by diminishing membership and too often divided against itself, has mounted a remarkably strong pushback, including demonstrations against investment firms that support privatization and threats to pull pension fund investments from those companies.[34] More than twenty major financial firms, including several that had publicly endorsed privatization, pulled out of COMPASS after hearing from their union clients, infuriating the White House.[35]

Bringing countervailing pressure out in the states and congressional districts are the AARP and its allies in the Campaign for America's Future, a broad coalition of labor, progressive, women's, and minority organizations. Those groups and many more have risen up together to save Social Security from those who have been pretending to rescue the program while seeking to destroy it. Americans United to Protect Social Security and dozens of other citizen groups have attracted support across the geographic, ethnic, ideological, and political boundaries that usually divide the nation.

Even rural and agricultural organizations that voted heavily Republican in 2004—such as the American Corn Growers Association and the National Farmers Union—have rejected the Bush privatization plan. The self-described conservative Republican who leads the corn farmers explained why he had joined Democrats and progressives to fight the President's plan.

"Social Security was one of the better-working programs the federal government ever did," he said, adding that he didn't see why rural Americans should support a plan they rightly regard as nothing more than "a way to get more money into the coffers of corporations."[36]

The cold reception that greeted Bush's message during the winter of 2004–2005 did not grow warmer in the ensuing months. His carefully staged town hall meetings did not attract voter support. Nor have fifty million dollars' worth of advertising and public relations campaigns mounted by his allies proved persuasive. Quite the reverse, apparently, since polls consistently show that opinions have shifted toward still firmer opposition to any form of privatization.[37]

By last summer, most Americans didn't believe the president's claim that his proposals would "save" Social Security. They didn't believe that his plan would improve the retirement income of workers or the program's finances. They didn't approve of the way he was handling the issue, registering their disapproval by an even larger margin than six months earlier. They didn't want to entrust their Social Security accounts to private management. They didn't want the system's guaranteed benefits to be cut.

President Bush holds up U.S. Treasury bonds as he tours the Bureau of Public Debt in Parkersburg, West Virginia, on April 5, 2005. At left is Susan Chapman, director of the division of federal investments. The president was in West Virginia to deliver remarks on his plans for privatizing Social Security.
(© AP Photo/Gerald Herbert)

## Wall Street's Inevitable Trillion-Dollar Windfall

Americans are often said to have a propensity to vote against their own economic interests, an assertion for which there is certainly a sizeable archive of evidence, including the reelection of George W. Bush and the Republicans who control Congress. Still they seem to understand that by abrogating the social insurance contract that has protected the great majority of Americans, the Republican leadership is seeking to reverse almost a century of progress.

Vindicating Franklin Roosevelt's faith in their wisdom, the American people evidently realize that the Bush Republicans are trying to sell them the raw deal to replace the New Deal. Why should anyone be surprised that they aren't buying?

# Conclusion

# Rejecting the Raw Deal and Strengthening Social Security

For years, George W. Bush has warned that Social Security is endangered by impending bankruptcy, expressing his deep concern about what that would mean for the nation. For months, he has proclaimed his determination to save and strengthen the program, vowing to prevail despite the political risk.

Bush has promised to replace the American social insurance system with private accounts that would earn great returns at minimal risk, with full rights of individual ownership and control. He has appointed a stacked commission to endorse his theories and led an intense, highly partisan, corporate-backed campaign to win public support for abolishing the system that has served Americans so well for the past seventy years.

The only thing Bush hasn't done is what the president of the United States is expected to do when he is seeking to change national policy: Draft specific proposals and send them up Pennsylvania Avenue to the Capitol. After five years in office, he has yet to adopt a complete, actuarially sound plan to deal with the supposed crisis that according to him threatens not only Social Security but America's future economic growth as well. If the situation is so urgent, why doesn't Bush propose a solution?

The answer, of course, is that the president and his advisers know that none of their schemes appeal to the majority of the American people, who strongly prefer to preserve Social Security and oppose privatizing, slashing, or dismantling it. In the White House they pretend never to look at polling data, but in fact they're painfully aware of the negative response to their ideas so far. For all their bold talk, they've left the job of proposing actual legislation to members of Congress, and they let them take the heat instead of Bush himself.

In fairness, the president has offered certain clues to the kinds of "reform" he would prefer even though he hasn't drafted any legislation. He vehemently objects to any tax increase. He wants private accounts carved out of Social Security revenues, and he wants to cut benefits sharply by using the "progressive indexing" plan proposed by Fidelity Investments vice president Robert Pozen (a privatization advocate who served on Bush's Social Security commission in 2001).[1]

Enacting those ideas as envisioned by Bush would inflict a horrific raw deal on American workers and their families.

The only remotely "progressive" aspect of the Pozen proposal is that it would maintain promised benefits for the 30 percent of workers at the lowest income levels. Everyone else, including workers with annual earnings as low as $35,000, would see their promised benefits cut sharply by a change in the way future benefits are calculated. Instead of indexing future benefits to wage increases, they would be indexed to price increases, which grow more slowly.[2]

Workers who earn $20,000 annually or less, not much above the poverty level, would still see their benefits calculated according to wage levels. Those earning higher incomes would see their benefits cut by increasing amounts along a sliding scale, up to $90,000, according to a mathematical formula that increases the relative influence of prices rather than wages.

Complex as that scheme may sound, the results would be starkly simple. An average wage earner retiring in 2045 would see his or her Social Security benefits cut by at least 16 percent; the same average earner retiring in 2075 would suffer a cut of at least 28 percent. The cuts could actually be considerably larger, since the Pozen plan would only close about 70 percent of the actuarial shortfall in Social Security revenues. Unless taxes are increased, the rest of the deficit would have to be covered with still more benefit cuts.

Should Congress ever enact the president's version of private accounts, those benefit cuts would be much larger—because every dollar diverted into a private account would have to be paid back in dollar-for-dollar benefit cuts plus inflation plus 3 percent. That's the fine print in the raw deal that Bush never mentions. Far from providing real ownership and independence, he would encourage workers to borrow money from their Social Security accounts to invest in the stock market on margin. At retirement, those borrowed funds would have to be paid back with interest and inflation. Anything left over would have to be used to purchase a fixed annuity (whose benefits, unlike Social Security, would not necessarily continue until death).

Now subtract those private account charges along with the Pozen plan cuts—and very little is left of the traditional Social Security benefit. In fact, almost nothing would be left for many middle- and higher-income wage earners.

Leaving aside the fact that all too many people depend on Social Security for most of their retirement income, the risks inherent in private accounts render that deal unacceptably bad.

How bad? Let's factor in Robert Shiller's estimate of future equity returns. Remember that Shiller is the distinguished Yale economist who warned of "irrational exuberance" among investors during the late 1990s and predicted the 2000 plunge in stock values. He believes that we would be unwise to expect a real return on investment of more than 4.6 percent.[3] Deduct that 3 percent claw-back, plus the fees and commissions charged by mutual fund management, and what would be left for most retirees equals less than the "return" on traditional Social Security.

And that equation doesn't include the enormous transitional costs of the private accounts, which would have to be made up with transfers from the Treasury's general revenues. That would mean substantial tax increases or huge budget cuts in other programs.

The White House has now grudgingly acknowledged that private accounts would do nothing to close the financing gap in Social Security that may occur between 2042 and 2052. Diverting those revenues would make the gap larger, as anyone who can do simple arithmetic would know. That has made it difficult to argue for privatization, whose prospects seem to have receded ever since Bush announced his intentions with great fanfare in his second inaugural address.

What's left without private accounts? Those accounts were meant to make up the difference between the benefits promised under current law and the reduced benefits provided to most retirees by "progressive indexing." For the conservatives who have always wanted to abolish Social Security and abhor fair taxation—including Bush—the fallback plan is evidently to reduce the program to a welfare benefit for the poorest workers. Everyone else would be left to the fortunes of the market, which would mean poverty and insecurity in old age for many Americans.

The president's "crisis" rhetoric, repeated and amplified by the conservative noise machine and the privatization lobby, has succeeded in convincing many Americans that Social Security faces serious financial problems. His wildly exaggerated doom-saying speeches conveniently omit any mention of far more pressing fiscal difficulties with the federal budget and Medicare costs—presumably because his policies have made them far worse. Believing his warnings about the eventual insolvency of Social Security—or believing that he believes them— would be easier if he hadn't inflicted such damage on the nation's finances.

The usual measurement of fiscal viability for Social Security is the outlook over the next seventy-five years, a number that reflects actuarial standards and is set down in statute. By that measure, Social Security is in reasonably good shape, especially when contrasted with the havoc wreaked by Bush on the federal budget and Medicare. According to the Social Security and Medicare trustees, Social Security's estimated shortfall amounts to 0.65 percent of the gross domestic product (GDP) between now and 2080. In 2004 dollars, that figure comes to $4.0 trillion.[4]

That sounds like a lot of money, until it is compared with the costs of the Bush legacy.

Over the same seventy-five-year period, the cost of the Bush tax cuts of 2001 and 2003—according to an analysis by the Center for Budget and Policy Priorities based on Congressional Budget Office estimates—is 1.99 percent of the GDP, or $12.3 trillion.[5] That happens to be exactly triple the Social Security deficit.

Then there's the additional burden Bush placed on Medicare, already imperiled by rising medical costs and an aging population, when he pushed through his prescription drug benefit (which was really a disguised subsidy to private health care companies). He claimed that his bill represented "reforms" that would save money, but the Medicare trustees think not. They project the cost of the drug benefit alone at $8.7 trillion, or 1.4 percent of the GDP, between now and 2080.[6] That's slightly more than double the Social Security shortfall.

Altogether, the price for the tax cuts and prescription drug benefit will amount to five times the projected deficit in Social Security over the actuarial period. And as the economists at the Center for Budget and Policy Priorities have pointed out, those estimates are quite conservative. Substitute the more optimistic Social Security data prepared by the Congressional Budget Office—which estimates the program's shortfall at only 0.4 percent of GDP[7]—and the difference enlarges to a factor of ten.

That's right: Bush is responsible for projected budgetary deficits that total at least five times and up to ten times the amount of the Social Security problem that supposedly worries him so much. Moreover, his plan—"progressive indexing" plus private accounts—would close only 24 percent of the estimated shortfall in Social Security revenues between now and 2080.

That suggests the Bush agenda has been shaped by right-wing ideology, not fiscal integrity.

What all those numbers also reveal is that the Bush Republicans are wrong about how to "save and strengthen" Social Security. It doesn't require privatization, which would actually worsen the fiscal shortfall by taking money out of the system. It doesn't require drastic cuts. According to most economic projections, including those of the trustees and the Congressional Budget Office, it may require no significant changes at all—depending on the nation's future economic growth. Should more pessimistic estimates about growth prove accurate, however, Social Security can be brought back into actuarial balance with relatively small changes in benefits and taxes.

Economist Peter R. Orszag, who is one of the nation's preeminent experts on Social Security, says there is no reason to ruin the system with private accounts or huge benefit cuts. "Social Security is like a car with a flat tire. We should fix the tire . . . not borrow the money to buy a new car."[8]

Orszag's automotive analogy makes perfect sense. And considering what Bush has done to Medicare and the federal deficit, there is a powerful argument for making no changes at all in Social Security until we have dealt with those issues. Certainly there is no reason for Democrats and other defenders of Social Security to negotiate with Bush as long as he keeps pretending that reform means privatization.

As a political matter, though, Social Security's defenders must be prepared to say how they think potential shortfalls in revenue should be met. What could be done to maintain all the benefits of Social Security, including the social insurance provided to widows and children, while bringing the system into actuarial balance beyond 2080?

Orszag and Peter A. Diamond, his colleague at the Brookings Institution, a centrist Washington think tank, have devised a "balanced plan" for restoring actuarial balance over the long term. As strong advocates of Social Security's historic structure, they believe that Congress should act to ensure real reform "sooner rather than later."

Orszag and Diamond call their plan balanced because it includes both modest increases in taxes and limited benefit reductions. Unlike the Pozen proposal, their plan is truly progressive because it would lift the level of maximum taxable earnings and reduce benefits most for those who are least likely to be affected by such cuts. These adjustments would be made gradually, along with additional changes that reflect longer life spans. They would slowly increase the employee share of the payroll tax by 0.9 percent over the fifty-year period between 2005 and 2055.[9]

The Brookings economists would also impose what they call a "legacy tax" on income that otherwise escapes FICA and benefit reductions for all persons becoming eligible for Social Security after 2023. And like other real reform proposals, their plan calls for inclusion of all newly hired municipal, county, and state government employees in Social Security. Until now, several million government workers have been segregated into separate pension plans and thus exempted from FICA taxation.[10]

The Orszag–Diamond plan suggests very limited, fairly distributed benefit reductions that would preserve Social Security as a social insurance system and maintain its actuarial balance well beyond seventy-five years. It would actually improve disability and survivor benefits and enhance benefits for the lowest earners. It would impose no changes on workers who are now fifty-six or older. Younger workers with average earnings would see some cuts, but they would be comparatively small—and over the long run, even younger workers whose benefits would be cut more still end up with larger real retirement incomes than under other plans—because their lifetime career earnings will also be considerably higher.

As Orszag and Diamond readily acknowledge, their "balanced" plan is hardly the only possible alternative. There are many other ways to distribute future burdens and benefits without privatization or harsh reductions.

Former Social Security commissioner Robert Ball—who served in the Kennedy, Johnson, and Nixon administrations and also sat on the Greenspan commission in 1983—has proposed a different combination of revenue and benefit adjustments that would preserve and fortify the system. Ball would slowly raise the cap on taxable earnings to restore coverage of 90 percent of all income, rather than the 85 percent now taxed. He would freeze scheduled reductions in the estate tax, requiring the likes of Paris Hilton to pay taxes on any inheritance of more than $3.5 million (or $7 million per couple). Rather than eliminating the estate tax, as Bush is seeking to do, Ball would reform it and dedicate the proceeds to Social Security.[11]

His plan would reduce future benefits by applying a more accurate consumer price index, which would slow down increases in the system's cost-of-living adjustment. He also would require all new state and local employees to be covered (and taxed) under Social Security.

More controversially, Ball would place a portion of Social Security revenues in equity markets, thus increasing the earnings that are otherwise restricted

Cartoon, 1936, by Clarence D. Batchelor. (© *The Granger Collection, New York*)

by Treasury bond rates. That is far less radical than it sounds—since every other public pension system, from New York to California, already invests directly in the stock market without inflicting any harm on capital markets.

## Rejecting the Raw Deal and Strengthening Social Security

There are, in short, many reasonable alternatives to the raw deal—and those alternatives are both more decent and more financially sound than the schemes that have emerged to date from the Cato Institute, the Bush White House, and the Republicans in Congress. Survey data show that most Americans prefer increasing the cap on FICA taxes to any other plan for preserving Social Security, so there is no political reason to fear proposals that restore the fairness that Bush wants to erase from America's political economy.

There could be no better way to celebrate the seventieth anniversary of the greatest government program the nation has ever known.

# Notes

## INTRODUCTION

1. Elisabeth Bumiller, "Traces of Terror: The Strategy; Bush Aides Set Strategy to Sell Policy on Iraq," *New York Times*, September 7, 2002.
2. Michel Tanner, "Social Security: Where's the Real Risk?" congressional testimony, June 30, 1998.
3. Jim Drinkard, "Poll: Social Security Plan Support Drops," *USA Today*, March 2, 2005.
4. Susan Page, "Poll: Tap Wealthy on Social Security," *USA Today*, February 9, 2005.
5. Editorial, "The Fright Mail Gambit," *New York Times*, November 30, 1992.
6. Glen Justice, "A New Target for Advisers to Swift Vets," *New York Times*, February 21, 2005.
7. Kenneth S. Davis, *FDR: The New Deal Years 1933–1937, A History* (New York: Random House, 1986), p. 505.
8. Laura Braden Dlugacz, "Progress for America Launches March Social Security Media and Grassroots Blitz," www.progressforamerica.com, March 17, 2005.
9. Bob Brigham, "Phasing Out Social Security," www .thereisnocrisis.com, March 4, 2005.
10. See, e.g., General Hugh S. Johnson, "A Hokus-Pokus: The Social Security Tax," *Vital Speeches of the Day*, December 1, 1937, pp. 116–117; John T. Flynn, "The Social Security 'Reserve' Swindle," *Harper's* (February 1939): 238–248.
11. Presidential Papers of Dwight David Eisenhower, Document #1147, "To Edgar Newton Eisenhower," November 8, 1954.
12. Sydney Blumenthal, "Recycled Rhetoric," *Salon.com*, March 3, 2005.

13. Address on behalf of Senator Barry Goldwater, "A Time for Choosing," October 27, 1964.

## 1 WHAT THE BUSH REPUBLICANS REALLY WANT

1. Acceptance speech as the 1964 Republican presidential candidate.
2. Letter from President Eisenhower to his brother, Edgar Newton Eisenhower, on November 8, 1954; www.eisenhowermemorial.org/presidential-papers/first-term/documents/1147.cfm.
3. Arnold Forster and Benjamin R. Epstein, *Danger on the Right* (New York: Random House, 1964), p. 136.
4. Bill Minutaglio, *First Son: George W. Bush and the Bush Family Dynasty* (New York: Random House, 1999), p. 83.
5. Memo from the Luntz Research Companies to Republicans in Congress, "Part VII: Social Security = Retirement Security," p. 100.
6. Ibid.
7. Ibid.
8. Seminar luncheon, "Social Security and the Future of Limited Government," sponsored by Cato on Thursday May 12, 2005, at the Waldorf-Astoria Hotel in New York City.
9. Various publications from the Cato Institute, www.cato.org.
10. Ron Suskind, "The Free-Lunch Bunch: The Bush Team's Secret Plan to 'Reform' Social Security," http://slate.msn.com, February 27, 2004.
11. Amity Shlaes, "O'Neill Lays Out Radical Vision for Tax," *Financial Times*, May 19 and 22, 2001.
12. Paul Krugman, "The Tax Cut Con," *New York Times*, September 14, 2003.
13. Laura Blumenfield, "Sowing the Seeds of GOP Domination; Conservative Norquist Cultivates Grass Roots," *Washington Post*, January 12, 2004.
14. David Brock, *The Republican Noise Machine: Right-Wing Media and How It Corrupts Democracy* (New York: Crown, 2004), p. 50.

# Notes

15. Ibid.
16. Grover Norquist, president of Americans for Tax Reform, National Public Radio, *Morning Edition*, May 25, 2001.
17. "An Arrangement Involving Two Indian Tribes, the Head of an Anti-Tax Organization and a Lobbyist Now under Criminal Investigation," *Associated Press*, June 8, 2005.
18. www.issues2000.org/George_W_Bush_Social_Security.htm.
19. Ramesh Ponnuru, "Taking on the Biggest," *National Review*, June 5, 2000.

## 2 THE PRESIDENT'S COMMISSION TO PRIVATIZE SOCIAL SECURITY

1. Knight Ridder, May 2, 2001.
2. Richard W. Stevenson, "For Bush, a Long Embrace of Social Security Plan," *New York Times*, February 27, 2005.
3. Ibid.
4. Paul Weyrich, "Blue Collar or Blue Blood? The New Right Compared to the Old Right," in *The New Right Papers*, ed. Robert Whitaker (New York: St. Martins, 1982).
5. Forster and Epstein, *Danger on the Right*, p. 182.
6. William Niskanen, "Environmental Policy: A Time for Reflection," *Regulation*, www.cato.org.
7. Radley Balko, "Hike in Cigarette Tax Opens Door to Other Vices," www.cato.org, April 7, 2004.
8. See www.cato.org/research/regulatory-studies/.
9. Stuart Butler and Peter Germanis, "Achieving a 'Leninist' Strategy," *Cato Journal* (1983).
10. Ibid.
11. Ibid.
12. Robert Dreyfuss, "The End of Social Security as We Know It?" *Mother Jones* (November/December 1997).
13. Glenn Kessler, "Paving the Way for Privatizing Social Security," *Washington Post*, June 26, 2001.
14. Speech in St. Charles, Missouri, November 2, 2000.
15. Presidential debate, Boston, October 3, 2000.

16. George W. Bush, "A Defining American Promise," speech delivered at Rancho Cucamonga, CA, May 15, 2000, www.vote-smart.org/speech_detail.php?speech_id=3289&keyword=&phrase=&contain=.

17. James Dao and Frank Bruni, Associated Press, May 4, 2000.

18. Suskind, "The Free-Lunch Bunch."

19. Max Sawicky, http://maxspeak.org, April 7, 2005.

20. Cursor.org, "Grants to Economic Security 2000" and "Grants to National Development Council."

21. *Cato Policy Report* (July/August 2001), p. 3.

22. Dean Baker and Mark Weisbrot, "Bush Commission: No Social Security Crisis," Center for Economic and Policy Research.

## 3  UNDER THE ASTROTURF CARPET

1. C-SPAN, *Washington Journal*, July 15, 2004, www.c-span.org/ram/wj/071504.ram.

2. Joshua Holland, "Blackwashing: Scratch the Surface of a Black Conservative Group and You Find a Vast Right-Wing Conspiracy," July 21, 2004, http://gadflyer.com/articles/?ArticleID=173.

3. "Periscope," *Newsweek*, March 31, 2005.

4. *San Francisco Examiner*, February 8, 1998.

5. Glen Turpening, "The Time Is Now for Social Security Privatization," #212, *National Policy Analysis*, National Center for Public Policy Research, September 1998.

6. Peterson's comments came during an appearance on the November 29, 2004, edition of Fox News Channel's *Hannity & Colmes*, http://mediamatters.org/.

7. Liquin Liu and Andrew Rettenmaier, "Social Security and Race," NCPA Policy Report #236, December 2000, www.ncpa.org/pub/st/st236/.

8. William W. Beach and Gareth E. Davis, "Social Security's Rate of Return," Center for Data Analysis Report #98-01,

# Notes

January 15, 1998; and William W. Beach and Gareth G. Davis, "Social Security's Rate of Return for Hispanic Americans," Center for Data Analysis Report #98-02, March 27, 1998.

9. Congressional Budget Office, *Administrative Costs of Private Accounts in Social Security* (Washington, D.C.: U.S. Government Printing Office, March 2004).

10. Steve Goss, deputy chief actuary, Social Security Administration, "Problems with 'Social Security's Rate of Return': A Report of the Heritage Center for Data Analysis," January 27, 1998, p. 1.

11. Ibid.

12. Statement of Cynthia M. Fagnoni, director, Income Security Issues, Health, Education, and Human Services Division, U.S. General Accounting Office, "Testimony before the Subcommittee on Social Security of the House Committee on Ways and Means, Hearing on the Impacts of the Current Social Security System—Reducing Poverty, Protecting Minorities, Surviving Families, and Individuals with Disabilities," February 10, 1999.

13. General Accounting Office, "Social Security and Minorities," April 2003.

14. Ibid.

15. Paul Krugman, "Little Black Lies," *New York Times*, January 28, 2005.

16. Terry M. Neal, "Blacks Give Social Security Plan Chilly Reception," *Washington Post*, May 16, 2005.

17. Edmund Andrews, "Clamor Grows in the Privatization Debate," *New York Times*, December 17, 2004.

18. Warren Vieth, "A Woman's Take on Social Security Overhaul," *Los Angeles Times*, March 30, 2005.

19. Stuart Butler and Peter Germanis, "Achieving a 'Leninist' Strategy," 1983.

20. Lawrence R. Jacobs, "UFO Stories: More Social Security Bunk," *New Republic* (1998).

21. "Third Millennium President Richard Thau Attends

White House Rose Garden Announcement of New Social Security Commission," press release, Third Millennium.

22. Marie F. Smith, president, and Bill Novelli, CEO, "Social Security: Where We Stand," open letter to AARP members, June 2005.

23. Bush rally in Albuquerque, New Mexico, March 22, 2005.

24. Barbara Basler, "Changing Social Security Is Risky Business: What Do Americans Think about Taking Money Out of Social Security for Private Accounts? It Depends on How Much They Know about the Risks," *AARP Bulletin* (February 2005).

25. Richard A. Viguerie and David Franke, *America's Right Turn: How Conservatives Used New and Alternative Media to Take Power* (Santa Monica, CA: Bonus Books, 2004).

26. Bill Berkowitz, "Richard Viguerie's Army Attacks Social Security," *Media Transparency*, March 9, 2005.

27. Ibid.

28. Deborah Solomon, "AARP's Antagonist," *New York Times Magazine*, March 13, 2005.

29. William March, "Holocaust Survivors Used in Florida Political Battle," *Tampa Tribune*, August 5, 1998.

30. www.dailykos.com/story/2005/4/10/12228/7430.

31. Steven T. Kessel, "Decision in the Case of Social Security Administration v. United Seniors Association," www.hhs.gov/dab/decisions/CR1075.html.

32. Nicholas Confessore, "Bush's Secret Stash," *Washington Monthly* (May 2004).

33. Maureen Dowd, "Swifties Slime Again," *New York Times*, February 24, 2005.

34. Glen Justice, "A New Target for Advisers to Swift Vets," *New York Times*," February 21, 2005.

## 4  WALL STREET'S INEVITABLE TRILLION-DOLLAR WINDFALL

1. CBO Testimony, statement of Douglas Holtz-Eakin, "The Future of Social Security," before the Special Committee

# Notes

on Aging, United States Senate, February 3, 2005.

2. Congressional Budget Office, *Social Security: A Primer* (Washington, D.C.: U.S. Government Printing Office, September 2001).

3. "FAQ on Social Security," on Cato website: www .socialsecurity.org/reformandyou/faqs.html.

4. William G. Shipman, "Private Social Security Accounts Are Best Long-Term Investment Despite Market Jitters," *New York Post*, August 14, 2002.

5. Michael Tanner, "The Better Deal: Estimating Rates of Return under a System of Individual Accounts," SSP #31, October 28, 2003.

6. Andrew Biggs, "Market Holds Little Risk for Social Security Accounts, *Buffalo News*, April 15, 2001.

7. Statement of Stephen Moore, director of Fiscal Policy Studies, Cato Institute, "Testimony before the Subcommittee on Social Security of the House Committee on Ways and Means: Hearing on the Future of Social Security for This Generation and the Next, Social Security Policy Experts," June 24, 1997.

8. James K. Glassman and Tyler Cowen, "The Death of Social Security: Debating Bush's Plan for Private Retirement Accounts, *Reason*, April 1, 2005.

9. Robert J. Shiller, "The Life-Cycle Personal Accounts Proposal for Social Security: An Evaluation," March 2005.

10. Ibid.

11. Robert J. Shiller, *Irrational Exuberance* (Princeton, NJ: Princeton University Press, 2000; 2nd ed., 2005).

12. "Berkshire's Buffett Praises AIG's Greenberg, Keeps Dollar Bet," Bloomberg.com, May 1, 2005.

13. Austan Goolsbee, "The Fees of Private Accounts and the Impact of Social Security Privatization on Financial Managers," University of Chicago, September 2004.

14. Jonathan Weisman, "The Politics of Social Security: Kerry to Use Study to Call Bush Plan a Wall Street Windfall," *Washington Post*, September 22, 2004.

15. Goolsbee, "The Fees of Private Accounts."
16. Stuart Butler and Peter Germanis, "Achieving a 'Leninist' Strategy," 1983.
17. The Bit Bucket, www.binarybits.org/archives/2005/01/fun_with_number.html, January 28, 2005.
18. Peter G. Peterson, "Social Security: The Coming Crash," *New York Review of Books*, December 2, 1982.
19. Robert Dreyfuss "The End of Social Security as We Know It?" *Mother Jones*, November 1, 1996.
20. Ibid.; Robert Dreyfuss, "The Biggest Deal," *American Prospect*, May 1, 1996.
21. William Greider, "The Man from Alcoa: Treasury Secretary Paul O'Neill Is Turning Out to Be a Dangerous Crank," *The Nation*, July 16, 2001.
22. *2001 Annual Report of the Board of Trustees of the Federal Old-Age and Survivors Insurance and Disability Insurance Trust Funds*, www.socialsecurity.gov/OACT/TR/TR01/index.html, March 19, 2001.
23. Lizette Alvarez, "In Campaigns Nationwide, Plans for Social Security Become Focus of Ads," *New York Times*, October 10, 2002.
24. See www.sourcewatch.org; and Jim Hightower, "Neutering Social Security," Louisville Jefferson County Democratic Party, http://louisvilledemocrat.com/updates.php.
25. Center for Public Integrity, www.publicintegrity.org/.
26. James Cramer, "Future Stock," *New York* magazine, January 3, 2005.
27. "Rove Uses Campaign Playbook to Mastermind Social Security Fight," Bloomberg.com, March 2, 2005.
28. Tom Hamburger, "Trade Groups Join Bush on Social Security," *Los Angeles Times*, April 11, 2005.
29. "Front Groups for the Attack on Retirement Security," http://www.aflcio.org.
30. Bloomberg News, "Business Groups Back Privatizing Social Security," January 21, 2005.

# Notes

31. Bennett Roth, "Social Security Lobbying War Is On; Costly, Partisan Bid Seen as Part 2 of 2004 Election," *Houston Chronicle*, February 14, 2005.
32. Tom Hamburger, "Trade Groups Join Bush on Social Security," *Los Angeles Times*, April 11, 2005.
33. Mark Silva, "Business, RNC Lend Hand to Bush Blitz: Aggressive Efforts to Guide Opinion Trends on Social Security Raise Concerns over 'Information-Sharing,'" *Chicago Tribune*, March 14, 2005.
34. See www.aflcio.org.
35. Ibid.
36. Bloomberg News, "Farm Groups Joining Democrats to Fight Bush on Social Security," June 15, 2005.
37. Pollingreport.com, "Social Security."

## CONCLUSION REJECTING THE RAW DEAL AND STRENGTHENING SOCIAL SECURITY

1. Robert Pozen, "A Social Security Plan for All," January 4, 2005.
2. Jason Furman, "An Analysis of Using 'Progressive Price Indexing' to Set Social Security Benefits," Center on Budget and Policy Priorities, May 2, 2005.
3. Robert J. Shiller, "The Life-Cycle Personal Accounts Proposal for Social Security: An Evaluation," Yale ICF Working Paper No. 05-06; Cowles Foundation Discussion Paper No. 1504, April 2005.
4. Richard Kogan and Robert Greenstein, "President Portrays Social Security Shortfall as Enormous, but His Tax Cuts and Drug Benefit Will Cost at Least Five Times as Much," *Center on Budget Policy and Priorities*, February 11, 2005.
5. Ibid.
6. Ibid.
7. Ibid.

8. "The New Proposal to Omit Several Trillion Dollars in Costs for Social Security Private Accounts," from the Federal Budget teleconference, December 14, 2004.

9. Peter R. Orszag and Peter A. Diamond, "Reforming Social Security: A Balanced Plan," Brookings Institution, December 2003.

10. Ibid.

11. Robert M. Ball, "Fixing Social Security," Century Foundation, May 3, 2005.

# Acknowledgments

Readers who are annoyed or even angered by this book should be aware that no one but me is to blame for mistakes, misspellings, and misconceptions. Readers who enjoy it should know, however, that I am indebted to many others for whatever may be useful or amusing in these pages.

This project began during a conversation with Charles Decker of PoliPointPress, and I remain grateful for his interest and for the introduction to his excellent colleagues, including Scott Jordan, Rhoda Dunn, Kelli Smith, Carol Pott, and Michael Bass. I owe particular thanks to Peter Richardson for his careful editing and thoughtful advice—and to John Sperling, whose founding of this new publishing venture is only his latest contribution to our country. I am very grateful to PoliPoint for providing the indispensable services of researcher Angie Crouse, whose swift, efficient, and cheerful labors made our rapid production schedule possible. I also have to thank copy editor, Laura Larson, for her diligent and flexible performance under trying circumstances.

I must try once more to express how much I appreciate my agents, Andrew Wylie and Jeffrey Posternak of the Wylie Agency. Their counsel and friendship sustain my work.

And I continue to appreciate the kind support of my colleagues at the *New York Observer*, including publisher Arthur Carter, editor Peter W. Kaplan, and city editor Terry Golway; at Salon.com, especially editors Joan Walsh, Geraldine Sealey, and Michal Keeley; and at *The American Prospect*, where editors Robert Kuttner and Michael Tomasky, as well as Barbara Saunders, Erin Pressley and other staff members, have been most helpful during this hectic time.

In putting together this book, I often turned to the writing of other reporters, bloggers, activists, and analysts. I depended on Joshua Micah Marshall's superb daily reporting on Talking Points Memo about the Bush privatization scheme. Among those who also provided inspiration and guidance are Eric Alterman, Don Babets, William Babiskin, Russ Bellant, Bill Berkowitz, Sidney Blumenthal, David Brock, Jonathan Chait, Norma Cohen, Robert Dreyfuss, E. J. Dionne, Nina Easton, Thomas Edsall, Kristofer Eisenla, Daniel Gross, Doug Henwood, Roger Hickey, Robert Kuttner, Richard Leone, Bill Minutaglio, Robert Parry, Sam Rosenfeld, Hans Riemer, David Sirota, Bob Somerby, Peter H. Stone, Ron Suskind, Ruy Teixeira, Michael Waldman, and Matthew Yglesias.

And I found important material on many websites and weblogs, notably Eschaton, Dailykos, ThereIsNoCrisis, Rawstory, Buzzflash, The Gadflyer, Media Transparency, PRWatch, and TAPPED.

# Acknowledgments

Lacking any graduate degrees, I relied heavily on the work of several outstanding economists, including Dean Baker, Brad DeLong, Peter Orszag, Max Sawicky, Robert Shiller, Gene Sperling, and Mark Weisbrot. I owe special thanks to Jason Furman, Paul Krugman, and Nomi Prins.

I found very useful material in the archives of Media Matters for America, Fairness and Accuracy in Reporting, the Campaign for America's Future, the Center for Tax Justice, the Center on Budget and Policy Priorities, the Center for Media and Democracy, the Center for American Progress, the Economic Policy Institute, the Brookings Institution, and the Century Foundation's Social Security Network.

I am obliged to Al Franken and James Roosevelt Jr. for their generous contributions and to Ben Wikler for his assistance.

I could not have completed this book without the patient support of many friends and members of my extended family, but I would be remiss if I failed to mention Julie Conason and Geoff Bryant, Teddy Gross and Ruth Nass, Gail Furman, Wally and Celia Gilbert, Alan and Susan Kahn, Andrew Karsch and Nan Richardson, Symmie and John Newhouse, and John R. Wagley Sr.

My wife Elizabeth Wagley is, of course, the most patient and devoted supporter of all, and the reader whose criticism and praise I value above all. I know how incredibly fortunate I am to have a loving partner who believes so strongly in what I do and yet doesn't hesitate to inform me promptly of my errors. Without her, very little would get done— and none of it would be as much fun.

# Index

# Index

# About the Author

**Joe Conason** is national correspondent for the *New York Observer*, where he writes a weekly column distributed by Creators Syndicate. He is also a columnist for Salon.com and the investigative editor for *The American Prospect* magazine.

His books *Big Lies: The Right-Wing Propaganda Machine and How It Distorts the Truth* and *The Hunting of the President: The Ten-Year Campaign to Destroy Bill and Hillary Clinton*, with Gene Lyons, were both national bestsellers.

His writing and reporting have appeared in many publications, including *Harper's*, *The Guardian*, *The Nation*, and *The New Republic*. He also appears frequently on television and radio (notably as a regular Friday guest on Air America's *The Al Franken Show*). He lives with his wife in New York City.